D0778565

ABIGAIL ADAMS

ABIGAIL ADAMS

ANGELA OSBORNE

AUG 1995
SALINAS PUBLIC LIBRARY

AL
JB
Adams

CHELSEA HOUSE PUBLISHERS

NEW YORK · PHILADELPHIA

Chelsea House Publishers
EDITOR-IN-CHIEF: Nancy Toff
EXECUTIVE EDITOR: Remmel T. Nunn
MANAGING EDITOR: Karyn Gullen Browne
COPY CHIEF: Juliann Barbato
PICTURE EDITOR: Adrian G. Allen
ART DIRECTOR: Maria Epes
MANUFACTURING MANAGER: Gerald Levine

American Women of Achievement
SENIOR EDITOR: Constance Jones

Staff for ABIGAIL ADAMS
TEXT EDITOR: Marian W. Taylor
COPY EDITOR: Terrance Dolan
DEPUTY COPY CHIEF: Ellen Scordato
EDITORIAL ASSISTANT: Theodore Keyes
PICTURE RESEARCHER: Andrea Reithmayr
ASSISTANT ART DIRECTOR: Laurie Jewell
DESIGN: Design Oasis
ASSISTANT DESIGNER: Donna Sinisgalli
PRODUCTION COORDINATOR: Joseph Romano
COVER ILLUSTRATOR: Bradford Brown

Copyright © 1989 by Chelsea House Publishers, a division of Main
Line Book Co. All rights reserved. Printed and bound in the
United States of America.

5 7 9 8 6 4

Library of Congress Cataloging in Publication Data

Osborne, Angela. ABIGAIL ADAMS.

(American women of achievement)
Bibliography: p.
Includes index.
Summary: Chronicles the life and achievements of the wife of the
second president of the United States.
1. Adams, Abigail, 1744–1818—Juvenile literature.   2. Presidents—
United States—Wives—Biography—Juvenile literature.   [1. Adams,
Abigail, 1744–1818.   2. First ladies]   I. Title.   II. Series.
E322.1.A38082   1988   973.4′4 [92]   88-1034
ISBN 1-55546-635-4
     0-7910-0405-8 (pbk.)

CONTENTS

AMERICAN WOMEN of ACHIEVEMENT

Abigail Adams
women's rights advocate

Jane Addams
social worker

Louisa May Alcott
author

Marian Anderson
singer

Susan B. Anthony
woman suffragist

Ethel Barrymore
actress

Clara Barton
founder of the American Red Cross

Elizabeth Blackwell
physician

Nellie Bly
journalist

Margaret Bourke-White
photographer

Pearl Buck
author

Rachel Carson
biologist and author

Mary Cassatt
artist

Agnes De Mille
choreographer

Emily Dickinson
poet

Isadora Duncan
dancer

Amelia Earhart
aviator

Mary Baker Eddy
founder of the Christian Science church

Betty Friedan
feminist

Althea Gibson
tennis champion

Emma Goldman
political activist

Helen Hayes
actress

Lillian Hellman
playwright

Katharine Hepburn
actress

Karen Horney
psychoanalyst

Anne Hutchinson
religious leader

Mahalia Jackson
gospel singer

Helen Keller
humanitarian

Jeane Kirkpatrick
diplomat

Emma Lazarus
poet

Clare Boothe Luce
author and diplomat

Barbara McClintock
biologist

Margaret Mead
anthropologist

Edna St. Vincent Millay
poet

Julia Morgan
architect

Grandma Moses
painter

Louise Nevelson
sculptor

Sandra Day O'Connor
Supreme Court justice

Georgia O'Keeffe
painter

Eleanor Roosevelt
diplomat and humanitarian

Wilma Rudolph
champion athlete

Florence Sabin
medical researcher

Beverly Sills
opera singer

Gertrude Stein
author

Gloria Steinem
feminist

Harriet Beecher Stowe
author and abolitionist

Mae West
entertainer

Edith Wharton
author

Phillis Wheatley
poet

Babe Didrikson Zaharias
champion athlete

CHELSEA HOUSE PUBLISHERS

"Remember the Ladies"

MATINA S. HORNER

Remember the Ladies." That is what Abigail Adams wrote to her husband
John, then a delegate to the Continental Congress, as the Founding Fathers
met in Philadelphia to form a new nation in March of 1776. "Be more generous
and favorable to them than your ancestors. Do not put such unlimited power
in the hands of the Husbands. If particular care and attention is not paid to
the Ladies," Abigail Adams warned, "we are determined to foment a Rebellion,
and will not hold ourselves bound by any Laws in which we have no voice,
or Representation."

   The words of Abigail Adams, one of the earliest American advocates of
women's rights, were prophetic. Because when we have not "remembered
the ladies," they have, by their words and deeds, reminded us so forcefully
of the omission that we cannot fail to remember them. For the history of
American women is as interesting and varied as the history of our nation as
a whole. American women have played an integral part in founding, settling,
and building our country. Some we remember as remarkable women who—
against great odds—achieved distinction in the public arena: Anne Hutchinson, who in the 17th century became a charismatic religious leader; Phillis
Wheatley, an 18th-century black slave who became a poet; Susan B. Anthony,
whose name is synonymous with the 19th-century women's rights movement,
and who led the struggle to enfranchise women; and, in our own century,
Amelia Earhart, the first woman to cross the Atlantic Ocean by air.

These extraordinary women certainly merit our admiration, but other women, "common women," many of them all but forgotten, should also be recognized for their contributions to American thought and culture. Women have been community builders; they have founded schools and formed voluntary associations to help those in need; they have assumed the major responsibility for rearing children, passing on from one generation to the next the values that keep a culture alive. These and innumerable other contributions, once ignored, are now being recognized by scholars, students, and the public. It is exciting and gratifying to realize that a part of our history that was hardly acknowledged a few generations ago is now being studied and brought to light.

In recent decades, the field of women's history has grown from obscurity to a politically controversial splinter movement to academic respectability, in many cases mainstreamed into such traditional disciplines as history, economics, and psychology. Scholars of women, both female and male, have organized research centers at such prestigious institutions as Wellesley College, Stanford University, and the University of California. Other notable centers for women's studies are the Center for the American Woman and Politics at the Eagleton Institute of Politics at Rutgers University; the Henry A. Murray Research Center for the Study of Lives, at Radcliffe College; and the Women's Research and Education Institute, the research arm of the Congressional Caucus on Women's Issues. Other scholars and public figures have established archives and libraries, such as the Schlesinger Library on the History of Women in America, at Radcliffe College, and the Sophia Smith Collection, at Smith College, to collect and preserve the written and tangible legacies of women.

From the initial donation of the Women's Rights Collection in 1943, the Schlesinger Library grew to encompass vast collections documenting the manifold accomplishments of American women. Simultaneously, the women's movement in general and the academic discipline of women's studies in particular also began with a narrow definition and gradually expanded their mandate. Early causes such as woman suffrage and social reform, abolition and organized labor were joined by newer concerns such as the history of women in business and the professions and in politics and government; the study of the family; and social issues such as health policy and education.

Women, as historian Arthur M. Schlesinger, jr., once pointed out, "have constituted the most spectacular casualty of traditional history. They have made up at least half the human race, but you could never tell that by looking at the books historians write." The new breed of historians is remedying that omission. They have written books about immigrant women and about working-class women who struggled for survival in cities and about black women who met the challenges of life in rural areas. They are telling the stories of women who, despite the barriers of tradition and economics, became lawyers and doctors and public figures.

The women's studies movement has also led scholars to question traditional interpretations of their respective disciplines. For example, the study of war has traditionally been an exercise in military and political analysis, an examination of strategies planned and executed by men. But scholars of women's history have pointed out that wars have also been periods of tremendous change and even opportunity for women, because the very absence of men on the home front enabled them to expand their educational, economic, and professional activities and to assume leadership in their homes.

The early scholars of women's history showed a unique brand of courage in choosing to investigate new subjects and take new approaches to old ones. Often, like their subjects, they endured criticism and even ostracism by their academic colleagues. But their efforts have unquestionably been worthwhile, because with the publication of each new study and book another piece of the historical patchwork is sewn into place, revealing an increasingly comprehensive picture of the role of women in our rich and varied history.

Such books on groups of women are essential, but books that focus on the lives of individuals are equally indispensable. Biographies can be inspirational, offering their readers the example of people with vision who have looked outside themselves for their goals and have often struggled against great obstacles to achieve them. Marian Anderson, for instance, had to overcome racial bigotry in order to perfect her art and perform as a concert singer. Isadora Duncan defied the rules of classical dance to find true artistic freedom. Jane Addams had to break down society's notions of the proper role for women in order to create new social institutions, notably the settlement house. All of these women had to come to terms both with themselves and with the world in which they lived. Only then could they move ahead as pioneers in their chosen callings.

Biography can inspire not only by adulation but also by realism. It helps us to see not only the qualities in others that we hope to emulate, but also, perhaps, the weaknesses that made them "human." By helping us identify with the subject on a more personal level they help us to feel that we, too, can achieve such goals. We read about Eleanor Roosevelt, for instance, who occupied a unique and seemingly enviable position as the wife of the president. Yet we can sympathize with her inner dilemma: an inherently shy woman, she had to force herself to live a most public life in order to use her position to benefit others. We may not be able to imagine ourselves having the immense poetic talent of Emily Dickinson, but from her story we can understand the challenges faced by a creative woman who was expected to fulfill many family responsibilities. And though few of us will ever reach the level of athletic accomplishment displayed by Wilma Rudolph or Babe Zaharias, we can still appreciate their spirit, their overwhelming will to excel.

A biography is a multifaceted lens. It is first of all a magnification, the intimate examination of one particular life. But at the same time, it is a wide-angle lens, informing us about the world in which the subject lived. We come away from reading about one life knowing more about the social, political, and economic fabric of the time. It is for this reason, perhaps, that the great New England essayist Ralph Waldo Emerson wrote, in 1841, "There is properly no history: only biography." And it is also why biography, and particularly women's biography, will continue to fascinate writers and readers alike.

ABIGAIL ADAMS

Abigail Adams, 22, gazes serenely from Benjamin Blyth's 1766 portrait. One observer called her expression "confident, controlled, and commanding."

ONE

The Die Is Cast

By April 19, 1775, everybody in New England knew trouble was coming. In Boston, British troops were digging trenches and mounting cannon. In the countryside, Americans were stockpiling muskets and ammunition. Meeting in Philadelphia a few months earlier, the Continental Congress had accused Britain of tyranny. In London, statesman William Pitt had warned that Britain and America were "in martial array, waiting for the signal to engage in a contest."

Nevertheless, April 19 dawned clear and cool in Braintree (now Quincy), Massachusetts, and Abigail Adams was serene. With her on the family farm were her four strong, healthy children and her beloved husband, John, newly returned after a long stay in Philadelphia. The fields around the farmhouse were turning green, the fruit trees were budding, and the sky was bright. On this quiet morning in Braintree, war seemed a distant prospect.

Just over the horizon, however, it was becoming a reality. Twenty miles away, in Lexington and Concord, gunfire was shattering the stillness of the New England morning. The Adamses, along with their neighbors, soon learned of events that would change their lives—and the course of history—forever.

On April 18, General Thomas Gage, commander of the British garrison in Boston, had learned that American patriots were storing gunpowder at Concord. Planning to take the arsenal by surprise, Gage secretly dispatched 1,000 of his red-coated soldiers to the village, 18 miles from Boston. But American patriots learned of the plan; during the night, horsemen Paul Re-

Abigail and John Adams's home (left) in Braintree, Massachusetts, was 20 miles from Lexington, site of the American Revolution's first battle.

vere and William Dawes raced through nearby towns and villages, warning their neighbors of the British advance.

The redcoats reached Lexington, on the road to Concord, the next morning. There, several dozen minutemen—farmers who could be ready for any emergency "at a minute's notice"—were lined up on the village green. "Disperse, ye rebels, disperse!" shouted the redcoats' officer. Suddenly, a shot rang out. To this day no one knows who fired it, but within a short time eight Americans lay dead on the green.

The British marched on to Concord, where they engaged in a brief skirmish with some 350 minutemen. As they hurried back to Boston, they were raked by gunfire from farmers hidden behind rocks, trees, and fences. By the end of the day the British had lost three times as many men as the Americans. The American Revolution had begun.

Before the British could spread their version of the day's events, the Americans had circulated their own: The battle of Lexington and Concord, they said, was an unprovoked massacre of peaceful farmers and an act of war. Like many other Americans, Abigail Adams and her husband must have heard the news with mixed emotions: grief for their fallen neighbors, combined with relief that the long-dreaded crisis had finally come to pass.

Few women in the American colonies, in fact, had more reason to expect the crisis than Abigail Adams. She shared an extraordinarily close relationship with her husband, not only in family matters but in the affairs of state in which he played a leading role. In the months before the outbreak of war, John Adams had been away from his wife for long periods, but the two often exchanged lengthy letters. As a Massachusetts delegate to the Continental Congress, he had spent most of the fall of 1774 in Philadelphia, helping to shape the future course of the American colonies.

Writing to her husband in Philadelphia, Abigail Adams had expressed her fears of impending war. "The great anxiety I feel for my Country, for you and for our family renders the day tedious, and the night unpleasant," she confided. "The Rocks and quick Sands appear upon every Side ... uncertainty and expectation leave the mind great Scope."

(The 18th century lacked formal rules for spelling, punctuation, and capitalization; writers and speakers used whatever forms struck them as appropriate. For the convenience of today's readers, this book will present the words of Adams, her family, friends, and associates in the style of the 20th century, modernizing the inconsistent and sometimes confusing grammar of the originals.)

John Adams had responded to his wife's fearful letter by reminding her that "resignation to the will of heaven is our only resource in such dangerous times" and urging her to make herself "as easy and quiet as possible." Recognizing that "the die is cast," Abigail Adams faced the future calmly. "We must expect continual alarms," she said, "and prepare ourselves for them." First, however, she had to prepare for another leave-taking. John Adams was expected back in Philadelphia at the end of April.

Abigail Adams faced a number of dilemmas in the spring of 1775. She hated the thought of war. "Did ever any kingdom or state regain their liberty when once it was invaded without bloodshed? I cannot think of it without horror," she wrote. At the same time, she understood that war is sometimes the price of liberty. "The sword," she said, "is now our only, yet dreadful, alternative."

Another of Adams's conflicts concerned day-to-day existence. John Adams was a lawyer, but he could earn no money at his profession while serving as a member of Congress, and

Shouting "The British are coming! The British are coming!" Paul Revere gallops through the Massachusetts countryside on the night of April 18, 1775.

congressional salaries were very small. In her husband's absence, then, Abigail Adams would have almost no income. And she would not only have to raise their four small children alone, she would have to manage the family farm by herself. She loved her husband, and she wanted him at her side, especially during the frightening days to come. But she also loved liberty and justice, and if John Adams could help his country retain them, she was willing to part with him for as long as necessary.

She had maintained this attitude since the day, five years earlier, that her husband had first been elected to the Massachusetts legislature. Because the British kept a close watch on colonial lawmakers, whom they regarded as radicals and potential traitors, the position was hazardous. John Adams had noted in his diary that although his wife "burst into a flood of tears" when she learned of his election, she insisted that he accept the honor. She was, he wrote, "very sensible of all the danger to her and to our children as well as to me, but she thought I had done as I ought. She was very willing to share in all that was to come and place her trust in Providence."

Redcoats and Minutemen exchange fire at the Battle of Lexington. The 1775 battle was followed by eight years of war between America and England.

New Englanders work in an 18th-century kitchen. Like other women of her time, Abigail Adams could weave cloth, churn butter, and cook over an open fire.

Deeply religious, Abigail Adams did put her trust in Providence—but she also had a strong sense of confidence in herself. In an era when women were expected to concentrate exclusively on their families and households, she cultivated an astonishingly wide range of intellectual interests, ranging from politics to philosophy to the future role of women in America. She was a traditional wife and mother, supplying her husband and children with powerful emotional and practical support, but she also expressed the radical idea that women should have "political, economic, and social rights equal to those of men."

During the American Revolution and the tumultuous years that followed, Abigail Adams would both record and help define American history. She would write hundreds of letters documenting her era, fearlessly express her opinions in private and in public, and serve as her husband's most trusted and influential political adviser.

On that fateful day in April 1775, Adams knew her country would face many perils on its road to independence. But she could not know how dark and dangerous that road would become, nor of the sacrifices and contributions she would make before the nation had reached its goal.

Unlike most of his colleagues, Reverend William Smith believed in female education. He encouraged his daughter Abigail to use his extensive library.

TWO

Learning the "Womanly Arts"

Abigail Smith was born on November 11, 1744, in Weymouth, a seacoast town south of Boston, Massachusetts. She was the second child born to Elizabeth Quincy Smith and her husband, the Reverend William Smith. Abigail was preceded by Mary, born in 1741, and followed by William in 1746 and Elizabeth in 1750.

William Smith, pastor of Weymouth's North Parish Congregational Church, had been born in Boston and educated at Harvard College. Like many clergymen of the time, he was also a part-time farmer, supervising the planting of crops on his land in Weymouth and on the two farms he owned near Boston. His wife, daughter of a wealthy Braintree family, traced her roots to New England's first settlers.

Both Elizabeth Smith and her husband were highly respected by Wey-

mouth's 2,000 residents, most of whom were farmers and members of the Congregational Church. William Smith was especially popular with his neighbors. Although he was one of Weymouth's most prosperous and best-educated citizens, he was easygoing and friendly, always ready to lend a hand or listen to the members of his flock. His daughter Abigail would later recall that her father often advised her to speak kindly, both to people and about them. He taught her, she said, "to say all the handsome things she could of persons, but not evil."

As the wife of a minister, Elizabeth Smith spent much of her time visiting the sick and bringing food, clothing, and fuel to needy families. From the time she was a little girl, Abigail accompanied her mother on these rounds of mercy. Elizabeth Smith taught her daughter that it was the duty of fortunate women to help those who were less fortunate, a lesson Abigail remembered all her life. Elizabeth also taught Abigail the skills then known as the "womanly arts": cooking, sewing, housekeeping, nursing, and vegetable gardening.

Because most New England schools of the time admitted only boys, girls were instructed at home. Few people believed that girls needed much learning; a woman who could read her Bible, write a plain letter, and do her household accounts was considered adequately educated. William Smith, however, thought otherwise. He loved his children and he loved books. What could be more natural than exposing one to the other? After Abigail learned the "Three Rs" (reading, 'riting, and 'rithmetic) from her mother, she started on her father's library.

Smith encouraged all his children to read, but Abigail was the most enthusiastic. Like her sisters, she was responsible for regular household chores, but whenever she had a free hour, she curled up in front of the fire with a book. She read history, sermons, philosophy, essays, and poetry. Still, she never learned elegant handwriting or Latin and Greek, which were considered essential for well-educated males. Although she eventually became one of the most well-read women in America, she was always sensitive about her lack of a formal education.

Abigail Smith was born and raised in this comfortable house in Weymouth, Massachusetts. Here, she first met her future husband, John Adams.

Watching her mother, a New England girl learns how to spin wool into thread. Elizabeth Smith carefully trained her daughters in such so-called womanly arts.

A pupil recites his lessons in an 18th-century classroom. When Abigail Adams was a girl, school enrollment was largely limited to boys.

Religious education was another matter. For the typical New Englander of the time, Sunday meant church—and nothing else. Services began in the early morning, halted for midday dinner, and resumed in the afternoon. The young Smiths, of course, were expected to set an example. From the time they were very young, they dutifully spent every Sunday in church, quietly listening to their father's long prayers and even longer sermons. In the Smith household, religion was more than an occupation for Sundays; it was the focus of daily life. Absorbing her parents' deeply felt convictions,

Abigail grew up with an unquestioning belief in God, a faith that remained strong throughout her life.

In some respects, young Abigail was a model child. Slender, small for her age, brown haired and wide eyed, she was shy, well mannered, and obedient. She was, however, far from being a small saint. Perhaps because she caught more childhood diseases than her siblings—and was consequently petted as a "delicate" child—she expected to get whatever she wanted.

Writing to a cousin, she once observed that "in youth, the mind is like a tender twig, which you may bend as

Colonial churchgoers listen to a lengthy sermon. As the daughter of a minister, Abigail Smith had to be especially well-behaved during Sunday services.

you please." Such a thought would have come as a surprise to Elizabeth Smith, who considered her daughter stubborn and hard to manage. Elizabeth's mother disagreed. She praised her granddaughter's self-reliance as well as her lively intelligence. "Wild colts make the best horses," said Grandmother Quincy. William Smith, too, admired his daughter's independent spirit. The opinions of Smith and his mother-in-law would soon be shared by a young lawyer from Braintree.

Abigail Smith was 15 years old when she first met 25-year-old John Adams. She left no record of her first reaction to the stocky, Harvard-educated attorney, but he recorded his early impression of her and her sisters in his diary. His observations were not flattering. "Are S. girls either frank or fond or even candid?" he asked himself. Answering his own question, he wrote, "Not fond, not frank, not candid." He did not even like their father, whom he called a "crafty, designing man."

Adams was not looking for a wife. He had, in fact, counseled himself against marriage, which, he noted in his diary, "might have depressed me to absolute poverty and obscurity to the end of my life." What Adams most wanted to avoid, he said, was "absolute idleness, or what is worse, gallanting [courting] the girls." He did, however, draw a written sketch of his idea of the perfect woman. She would be a person to whom "the highest pinnacle of glory" would be giving birth to a "hero or a legislator, a great statesman or divine [clergyman] or some other great character that may do honor to the world."

Two years after his first encounter with the Smiths, Adams visited the family with his friend Richard Cranch, who was engaged to Mary Smith. This time, his reaction to Abigail was altogether different. She was, he discovered, unlike any woman he had known. Pale, attractive, and gracious, she was also witty, surprisingly well read, and highly opinionated. Adams described her in his diary. "Tender feelings, sensible, friendly," he wrote. "Not a disagreeable word or action. Prudent, modest, delicate, soft, sensible, obliging, active." John Adams was falling in love.

Abigail Smith was strongly attracted to her new admirer, but she was cautious, too. She knew her choice of a husband would determine the course of her adult life. In 18th-century America and England, a married woman had no legal identity. As British jurist William Blackstone defined the marriage relationship, "The very being or legal existence of the woman is suspended during the marriage, or at least incorporated and consolidated into that of the husband, under whose wing, protection, and cover she performs everything."

Abigail Smith had no intention of "performing under the wing" of any

Richard Cranch, Abigail Smith's future brother-in-law, introduced her to John Adams in 1761. Three years later, Smith, then 19, married the 29-year-old Adams.

man who lacked respect for her individuality. She had been deeply impressed by the writings of Samuel Richardson, a British novelist who addressed the questions of personal identity, marriage, and the role of educated women. Richardson advanced the then shocking notion that unless a woman found a prospective mate who was as intelligent as she and who appreciated her accomplishments, she should reject marriage.

Smith agreed with Richardson, whom she called a "master of the human heart," but such mates as he described were rare. Responding to a friend's letter asking about interesting, eligible men, she wrote, "Why, I believe you think they are as plenty as herrings, when alas! There is [as] great [a] scarcity of them as there is of justice, honesty, prudence, and many other virtues."

John Adams seemed to be one of these rare specimens. Only slightly taller than herself (she was about five feet, seven inches tall) and somewhat overweight, he was not handsome by conventional standards. But, more important to Smith, he was dazzlingly intelligent and—if possible—even more argumentative than she. Adams became an increasingly frequent visitor to Smith's home, where the two spent hours discussing literature, politics, philosophy, and religion. But before many months had passed, most of their conversations were about marriage.

When Adams and Smith were unable to meet, they wrote letters. The young lovers were as candid in writing as they were face to face. After Smith told Adams she wanted his honest evaluation of her personality and actions, he responded with a long list of complaints: She read so much that her head hung "like a bulrush"; she did not sing or dance; she had formed the bad habit of sitting with her legs crossed, which ruined her posture.

Smith was undisturbed by the criti-

John Adams was 31 when he sat for this portrait by American artist Benjamin Blyth in 1766, two years after he and Abigail Smith were married.

cism. She replied that it was pointless to blame her for not singing, as her voice was "harsh as the screech of a peacock." Then, pretending to scold Adams, she said, "A gentleman has no business to concern himself about the legs of a lady." In another letter, Smith remarked that "courage is laudable [praiseworthy], a glorious virtue in your sex.... For my part, I think you ought to applaud me for mine." Adams responded by teasing her about her "unladylike habit of reading, writing, and thinking."

Not all the couple's letters were written in a joking tone. "My soul and body," said Adams to Smith, "have been thrown into disorder by your absence." He sometimes addressed her as "Miss Adorable" and talked of the "two or three million kisses" he wanted to give her. She thought about him "with the tenderest affection," and said that at night, "I no sooner close my eyes than some invisible being bears me to you." Her heart and his, she asserted, "were cast in the same mold."

On October 25, 1764, the Reverend William Smith presided over the wedding of his daughter Abigail, not quite 20 years old, and John Adams, 29. As wedding guests congratulated the couple in Weymouth, celebrants across the ocean were cheering another milestone: October 25 was the fourth anniversary of the coronation of Britain's King George III. In ways that no one could have predicted at the time, the participants of both celebrations would soon cross each other's paths with explosive consequences.

Still standing in Quincy (formerly Braintree), Massachusetts, is the house where Abigail and John Adams lived for the first 20 years of their marriage.

THREE

"We Never Can Be Slaves"

After their wedding, Abigail and John Adams moved to Braintree, the seacoast village where John had been raised and where his mother still lived. The couple's new residence, which John Adams had inherited from his father, was an 80-year-old house on 10 acres of farmland. On the first floor was a parlor, an office, a spacious kitchen built around an immense stone fireplace, and a small room for the housemaid. A steep wooden staircase led to two large bedrooms and two tiny, low-ceilinged children's rooms on the second floor. Above this was an attic.

The young couple settled happily into married life. Writing to a friend soon after her wedding, Abigail Adams compared her husband's presence to "sunshine"; he, in turn, called marriage "the source of all my felicity." In the first months of their marriage, the two were seldom apart. While John Adams worked on legal cases in his home office, his wife was busy in the kitchen, baking bread, stirring cornmeal-and-molasses puddings, or roasting meat on a spit in the fireplace.

Even with a servant to help her, Abigail Adams faced a formidable amount of housework. Along with cooking, there was sewing; she made all her own and her husband's clothes as well as their sheets, towels, and other linens. Water had to be carried in from the well, butter churned, meat and fish smoked or salted, the vegetable garden tended, the chickens fed, and the cows milked.

When John Adams was not reading his law books or preparing cases, he was caring for his livestock, planting crops, or pruning his apple trees, occupations he enjoyed thoroughly. Probably only half-joking, he said that

When Abigail Adams was young, a large wood-burning fireplace was essential kitchen equipment. Hooks suspended from a rod held cooking pots over the flames.

rather than practice law, he would prefer to "chop wood, dig ditches, and make a fence upon my poor little farm."

The Adamses were deeply in love. Despite their many chores, they found time for sleigh rides and long walks in the country, continuing the never-ending conversations they both cherished. And by their first summer together, they had something else to cherish: a baby girl. When little Abigail, who was always called "Nabby," arrived in July 1765, her parents were overjoyed. Nabby's "pretty smiles," wrote the ecstatic new mother, "already delight my heart." She called the

baby "the dear image of her still dearer pappa."

Meanwhile, John Adams was making a name for himself as an attorney. His growing law practice required frequent absences from Braintree. During these periods of separation, Abigail Adams relied for company, as she always had, on her books. One of her favorites was *Sermons to Young Women*, written by British clergyman James Fordyce. To modern readers, Fordyce, who accepted prevailing notions of male superiority, may seem like a strange choice for a woman like Adams. "Commerce, politics, exercises of strength and dexterity, abstract philosophy, the sciences and the like," he wrote, "are the proper province of men." What attracted Adams to Fordyce was probably his attitude about the female intellect.

A woman's mental accomplishments, asserted the clergyman, would remain long after her "girlish bloom" had faded. Admitting that "the softer sex" was not always given the respect or justice it deserved, he urged women to read and study as much as they could. Reading Fordyce's sermons strengthened Adams's determination to improve her mind.

As usual, Adams discussed her ideas with her husband. "I have often been tempted to believe," she said in one letter, "that [your heart] was made with a harder metal, and therefore less liable to an impression. Whether [both our hearts] have an equal quantity of steel, I have not yet been able to discover, but do not imagine that they are either of them deficient."

The Adamses also continued to share their ideas about political activity in the colonies, which was reaching a fever pitch by the time of Nabby's birth. Reporting from Boston, John Adams supplied his wife with up-to-the-minute news, answering what he teasingly called her "ten thousand questions." Crowding out other topics was a series of dramatic events that clearly foreshadowed a "contest" between England and its American possessions.

A New England woman and her daughter prepare a fire in their backyard smokehouse. Smoking was a common method of preserving meat in colonial days.

In 1765, Britain's Parliament, in which Americans had no voice, passed the Stamp Act. Imposing a tax on all printed matter in the colonies, from legal documents to newspapers to playing cards, the new law outraged Americans, and angry voices rang out in each of the 13 colonies. No one had the right to tax Americans but their own elected legislators, asserted America's patriots. The Stamp Act was a clear case of "taxation without representation."

John Adams knew that American resistance to the Stamp Tax could have dangerous results, both for his country

Sheltered by the "Liberty Tree," a huge elm that became a symbol of American defiance, Bostonians denounce British taxation without representation.

and his family. Without tax stamps, court business could not be legally transacted. Without the courts, lawlessness would prevail. Not only would colonial life be thrown into disarray, but Adams's thriving legal practice would end abruptly, leaving him with no way to support his wife and child. Nevertheless, he firmly believed that the colonists should refuse to buy "the king's stamps."

Adams's sentiments were shared by most colonial leaders. In the Virginia legislature, a representative named George Washington told his colleagues that the members of Parliament had "no more right to put their hands into my pocket, without my consent, than I have to put my hands into yours for money." Americans throughout the colonies banded together as "Sons of Liberty," forcing tax collectors to resign, burning the hated "stamp paper," and harassing unpopular officials. In Boston, furious mobs surged through the streets, hanging the stamp distributor in effigy and burning British officials' homes and offices.

Like most of their friends and neighbors, Abigail and John Adams were faced with a dilemma: Still considering themselves loyal British subjects, they were also determined to retain the rights of free citizens. "In all the calamities which have ever befallen this country," wrote John Adams, Americans had never "felt so great a concern . . . as on this occasion." The

Britain's George III was immensely popular with Americans until 1765, when he approved passage of the Stamp Act. Abigail Adams later called him a "wretch."

conversation of the young Adamses now centered almost exclusively on politics. They spent Christmas night, 1765, sitting by the fire, "thinking, reading, searching, concerning taxation without consent, concerning the great pause and rest in business," according to John Adams's diary.

Temporarily unemployed because of the Stamp Act crisis, Adams increased his political activities, writing articles,

Americans protest the Stamp Act—"The Folly of England and the Ruin of America"—with a thunderous torchlight parade in New York City.

attending debates, and joining the Sons of Liberty in Boston. After lengthy discussions with his wife, he published a newspaper article in which he urged Americans to assert their "rights and liberties" so that "the world may know . . . that we never can be slaves."

The intensity of the colonists' opposition to the Stamp Act took the British by surprise. Realizing it could not be enforced, Parliament repealed the act in the spring of 1766. At about the same time, John Adams was elected one of Braintree's selectmen (town officers). By the time he returned to his law practice, his writings and political activism had made him a well-known figure. The repeal of the Stamp Act brought calm to the colonies, at least for the moment.

By the spring, Abigail Adams and her daughter Nabby had recovered from severe attacks of whooping cough; the little girl was now cutting her first teeth and was, according to her proud mother, "fat as a porpoise." Work at the farm, however, was increasing. The Adamses now owned 3 cows, 4 horses, and 20 sheep, all of them Abigail Adams's responsibility. Also up to her was planning, cooking, and serving meals for her family and their guests. Eager to discuss law and politics with the now-famous John Adams, visitors had started flocking to the small house in Braintree. A well-trained New England hostess, Abigail Adams welcomed and fed them all.

Although she had plenty of company, Abigail Adams was lonesome for her sister Mary, who had recently moved to the town of Salem with her husband, Richard Cranch. "Tis a hard thing to be weaned from anything we love," Abigail wrote to her sister. "I think of you ten times where I used to once." She had longed to visit Salem, but her husband's nonstop political and business affairs kept her from making the 25-mile journey until the summer of 1766.

In August, she was finally able to write and tell her sister that she and her husband were ready to make the two-day trip. No longer, she said, would "mountains arise to hinder me." In characteristic style, she added, "Molehills I always expect to find, but them I can easily surmount." The sisters had a happy reunion in Salem, where politics, for once, did not hold center stage in all conversations. His wife and sister-in-law, recalled an amused John Adams in his diary, had a wonderful time talking about "ribbon, catgut and Paris net, riding hoods, cloth, silk, and lace."

Soon after her return to Braintree, Abigail Adams discovered that she was expecting another child. Through the winter and into the spring and summer, she took care of her home and baby as her husband continued to "ride circuit" (travel from one district courthouse to another). Both wife and husband complained about his frequent absences, but both knew they were necessary. "Nothing but the hope of acquiring some little matter for my dear family," wrote John Adams in his diary, "could carry me through these tedious excursions."

On July 11, 1767, Abigail Adams gave birth to a fine healthy baby. His parents named him John Quincy, after his mother's grandfather. Because John Adams was so often away from home, young John and his sister were largely raised by their mother. She, who had confessed to being bored by her

Patriots exchange rumors in a Boston coffeehouse. Barred by her sex from such meetings, Abigail Adams relied on her husband's reports for the latest news.

friends' "chit-chat" about their off-springs' bright sayings, now found herself in danger of doing the same thing. Somewhat to her surprise, she discovered that she truly enjoyed the company of her children. Their presence, she said in a letter to Mary, "twines round one's heart."

Sharing Boston Common in 1768 are dogs, cows, strolling citizens, and red-coated British troops, who used the city park as a drill field.

Meanwhile, the political pot continued to boil. Just as John Quincy Adams was born, Britain's Parliament announced the passage of the Townshend Acts, a new series of regulations and taxes regarded by the colonists as highly obnoxious. John Adams's absences from home now grew longer than ever; when he was not riding the circuit or pleading cases in the Boston courts, he was denouncing the Townshend Acts in Boston's coffeehouses. Finally, he and his wife decided to move to Boston. Abigail Adams liked living in Braintree, but she loved John Adams. When she moved to the city, she thought, she would once more have a husband, and her children a father.

In March 1768 the Adams family settled down in a big white house on Brattle Square. Boston, especially when compared to Braintree, was riotously noisy. Horse-drawn wagons rattled over the cobblestones; vendors shouted invitations to buy their fish, meat, and vegetables; boisterous crowds milled through the streets all day and all night. Directly across the street from the Adamses' house, two regiments of newly arrived British soldiers held daily drills, splitting the morning air with the shriek of fifes and the insistent thunder of drums.

Nevertheless, Abigail Adams found the new location invigorating. It was across the street from the Congregational Church and two blocks from the

Faneuil Hall was the scene of many prerevolutionary meetings. Often called the "Cradle of Liberty," the enlarged and renovated hall remains a Boston landmark.

Town House, site of Boston's government and courts. Nearby was the city's central marketplace and public auditorium, Faneuil (which rhymes with *Daniel*) Hall. Boston, which had a population of about 16,000 in 1768, was a lively and exciting place, the legal and political heart of the Massachusetts colony.

John Adams now spent much of his time at home, and his wife could also enjoy the company of relatives and friends who lived within walking distance. Among the frequent visitors to the Adams household were John's cousin, political activist Samuel Adams, and his wife, Betsey; legislator John Hancock; attorney James Otis; and the Adams's family doctor, Joseph Warren. Abigail Adams was especially fond of Warren, who was a witty, politically astute conversationalist as well as a skilled physician.

In December 1768, just after her 25th birthday, Abigail Adams gave birth to her 3rd child, a daughter named Susanna. Unlike her siblings, little "Suky" was frail and sickly from birth. Despite her parents' dedicated care and Dr. Warren's best efforts, she lived for only 14 months. Neither of her parents, grief stricken by the loss of their daughter, were ever able to talk or write about her. When she died, in February 1770, her mother was pregnant again.

Meanwhile, tension continued to rise. Bostonians resented the red-coated British soldiers—whom they tauntingly called "lobsterbacks"—stationed in their midst. The city buzzed with wild stories: Soldiers had raped a local woman, had killed a child, and were preparing to attack the civilian population. The rumors were false, but they kept the city in a state of jittery hostility.

On the cold evening of March 5, a crowd of men and boys began to exchange insults with British sentries at the Boston Custom House. The air was soon filled with flying snowballs, then rocks, then bullets. When the smoke cleared, five Americans lay sprawled in the snow; three were dead, two mortally wounded. News of the tragedy, which came to be known as the Boston Massacre, spread quickly. Church bells rang all over the city: voices screamed, "Fire!" In minutes, the streets were filled with running men, many of them carrying weapons.

At that moment, John Adams was attending a political meeting at a friend's house. In his diary, he recalled that when he and his companions heard the bells pealing, they assumed a fire had broken out and rushed into the street to help. Asking questions as he raced toward the center of the city, Adams learned of the bloodshed at the Custom House. His first thought, he remembered, was to get home to his wife, now almost seven months pregnant, and his two children. His cloak thrown over one shoulder, he dashed through the crowds of frightened and angry townspeople toward Brattle Square.

When he entered his house, Adams found a surprisingly peaceful scene. His wife, of course, had heard the shots, the bells, the shouting in the streets. She had been frightened but, she told her husband, there seemed to

British soldiers fire on a hostile Boston crowd. Five Americans died in the March 5, 1770, fray, which patriots immediately labeled a "massacre."

be only one sensible thing to do: Put the children to bed. Four-year-old Nabby had gone right to sleep, but Johnny, two and a half, had insisted on going out to see the excitement. He had finally retired, said his mother, but not without a struggle. John Adams was relieved to find his family safe and was both impressed and amused by his wife's matter-of-fact reaction to the crisis. As the city settled into an eerie silence, the two spent the rest of the evening talking about what would happen next.

After the Boston Massacre a British officer and eight soldiers were charged with murder. The city's rage had reached the boiling point, and the men narrowly escaped lynching at the hands of an angry mob. One after another, the city's lawyers—both British and colonial—refused to take their case. Defending redcoats was a dangerous business.

Both Abigail Adams and her husband believed that all people had the right to legal counsel and a fair trial. With his wife's approval, Adams volunteered to serve as defense attorney for the accused men. When the trial took place the following fall, he argued their case brilliantly. In spite of the open hostility of most Bostonians, 12 of whom sat on the jury, the British military men were found innocent of murder and released.

While Adams was preparing his case, two major events—one personal, one political—took place in his family's life. On May 29, Abigail Adams gave birth to another vigorous son, this one christened Charles by his delighted parents. His arrival, noted John Adams in his diary, seemed to restore Abigail's spirits, which had been at a low ebb since Susanna's death. Soon after Charles's birth, Adams was asked to run for the Massachusetts legislature. When he told his wife, she was first upset, then supportive. He doubted, however, that he would be elected, believing that his upcoming defense of the redcoat "murderers" had made him the most despised man in Boston.

He was wrong. When Boston's voters cast their ballots on June 6, John Adams was elected by a four-to-one majority. Amazed, he hurried home to tell his wife. Would she be distressed? His election, after all, meant that he would have less income and even less time to spend with his family. It would also leave him open to charges of treason by the British government.

Adams need not have worried. His "excellent lady," he noted in his diary, not only rejoiced in news of the election, but said she had never doubted its outcome. Declaring herself "very willing to share in all that was to come," she added that she "feared nothing but our parting." Future events would often force them to live apart from each other, but in the sense meant by Abigail Adams, she and the man she loved would never be parted.

Abigail Adams was a loving and supportive wife, but she was also a fiercely inde- pendent woman who insisted that her sex deserved "rights equal to those of men."

FOUR

"The Flame Is Kindled"

Abigail Adams was a study in contrasts. She believed that woman's proper role was that of wife and mother, yet she deeply admired women who went beyond those roles. She yearned for her husband's full-time company, but she urged him to accept assignments that kept him away from her. She insisted that simple pleasures were the best. "All that is necessary for man to know in order to be happy," she said, "is easily obtained." At the same time, she read avidly and longed to travel.

In a 1770 letter to her younger cousin, Isaac Smith, Jr., she said, "Had nature formed me of the other sex, I should certainly have been a rover." When Smith said he was considering a trip to England, she urged him to go. "Now is the best season of life for you to travel," she wrote him, "[before] you have formed [a] connection which would bind you to your own little spot." Smith took her advice, promising to write her, as she requested, about everything he saw that was "curious or remarkable."

When she read Smith's glowing reports of England and its vast cathedrals, ancient buildings, and colorful theaters, Adams was clearly envious. "From infancy," she confessed, "I have always felt a great inclination to visit the mother country." However, she added quickly, women were "considered domestic beings, and although they inherit an equal share of curiosity with the other sex . . . few are hardy enough to venture abroad."

In any case, she continued briskly, it was "almost impossible for a single lady to travel without injury to her character" because of "the natural tenderness and delicacies of our constitutions, added to the many dangers we

Intrigued by her cousin Isaac's descriptions of Westminster Abbey (pictured) and other English sights, Adams said she was tempted to become a "rover."

are subjected to from your sex." But she ended her letter on a wistful note: "And those who have a protector in a husband have, generally speaking, obstacles sufficient to prevent their roving."

The "obstacles" to Abigail Adams's roving increased in mid-1772. On September 15, Thomas Boylston Adams became the 6th member of the family, joining John, now 37; Abigail, 27; Nabby, 7; Johnny, 5; and 2-year-old Charlie. Tommy, as he was immediately nicknamed, was bald, round-cheeked, and solemn. He looked, said relatives and friends, much like his father. John Adams left no record of his opinion on this matter, but he clearly enjoyed the new baby, as he did all his children. Tommy's small, serious face, he noted, made him laugh whenever he looked at it.

Eight months later, no one was laughing. In May 1773, Parliament passed the Tea Act, a new law requiring American merchants to pay stiff taxes on tea whereas British merchants paid almost none. Because it would drive Americans out of the highly profitable tea trade and give Britain increased control over the colonies' economy, the act infuriated Americans. Tea was their favorite beverage, consumed in enormous amounts throughout the colonies. What right, they asked, had the British to control America's tea trade? No right at all, responded Sons of Liberty Sam Adams, Paul Revere, and John Hancock.

The British knew the Tea Act would be unpopular in the colonies, but they never expected the extreme reaction it produced: Tea-drinking America staged a boycott. Citizens throughout the colonies renounced their beloved beverage and switched to coffee and chocolate, although few found the change easy. "Tea must be universally renounced," wrote John Adams to his

Disguised patriots heave British tea into Boston Harbor on December 16, 1773. The rebellious act delighted Americans and outraged the British.

wife, adding grimly, "I must be weaned, and the sooner, the better." In November 1773, when 3 British merchantmen arrived in Boston Harbor with 342 chests of tea, political activists asked the Crown-appointed governor to send the tea-laden ships back to England. The governor refused. Clearly, trouble was brewing.

Like most Bostonians, Abigail Adams was both excited and worried. Writing to a friend on December 5, she said, "The tea, that baneful weed, is arrived. Great, and I hope effectual, opposition has been made to the landing of it. The proceedings of our citizens have been united, spirited, and firm. The flame is kindled and, like lightning, it catches from soul to soul. I tremble when I think what must be the direful consequences."

The consequences were not long in coming. On December 16, 1773, Bostonians attended a mass meeting to discuss the tea crisis. Suddenly, an Indian war whoop split the air. "To the docks!" shouted a thousand voices. At the waterfront, some 150 men, dis-

41

guised as Mohawk Indians, boarded the tea ships and pitched their precious cargo into Boston's icy harbor.

Patriots rejoiced at the news of the "Boston Tea Party." Abigail Adams called it a "most momentous" event, and her husband agreed. "This is the most magnificent move of all," he wrote in his diary. "This destruction of the tea is so bold, so daring, so firm ... that I must consider it an epoch in history." The British, predictably, took a different view. If they had been astonished by the tea boycott, they were dumbfounded by the tea party. When George III learned of it, he was outraged. "The die is now cast," he thundered. "The colonies must either submit or perish!"

Parliament ordered Boston to pay for the destroyed tea; Boston rejected the demand. In response, the British lawmakers issued a new set of laws, known to Americans as the "Intolerable Acts." The first closed the port of Boston, the next curtailed Massachusetts's powers of self-government, and the third forced residents to lodge British soldiers in their homes.

In May 1774, General Thomas Gage, the new governor of Massachusetts and commander in chief of British forces in America, arrived in Boston. His mission: to crush resistance to the Crown. Gage's first move was to seal the port; after June 1, nothing, including food, could be shipped into the city. Reflecting on this dismal state of

Bostonians were dismayed by the 1774 arrival of General Thomas Gage (shown here). Under his rule, predicted John Adams, the city would surely "suffer martyrdom."

affairs, John Adams wrote to his wife. "We live, my dear soul, in an age of trial," he said. "The town of Boston, for ought I can see, must suffer martyrdom. It must expire. And our principal consolation is that it dies in a noble cause: the cause of truth, of virtue, of liberty, and of humanity."

Writing to a friend in England, Abigail Adams painted an even darker picture: "We are invaded with fleets and armies, our commerce not only obstructed but totally ruined, the courts of justice shut, many driven out from the metropolis, thousands reduced to want or dependent upon the charity of their neighbors for a daily supply of food, all the horrors of civil war threatening us on one hand, and the chains of slavery ready forged for us on the other."

The recipient of this gloomy report was Catharine Macaulay, a radical British intellectual and political historian. Although Adams and Macaulay had never met face to face, they had mutual acquaintances and often shared their ideas through letters. Adams admired the unconventional Macaulay, who forcefully expressed her opinions about politics, current affairs, and other matters usually limited to men. Macaulay, who openly sympathized with the American colonists, was delighted to exchange correspondence with Adams, who offered firsthand news from Massachusetts, the center of America's revolutionary activity.

Another favorite Adams correspondent was an American woman, Mercy Otis Warren. Wife of James Warren, a prominent Massachusetts patriot and colleague of John Adams, Mercy Warren was a distinguished playwright and historian in her own right. Her first published work was *The Adulateur*, a satirical play that appeared in 1772. It was followed by more political comedies, including *The Defeat* and *The Group*, and much later, by the three-volume *A History of the Rise,*

Progress, and Termination of the American Revolution. The early satires were written under a male pen name; not even the outspoken Warren dared admit authorship of such "unfeminine" material.

When Adams and Warren first met in 1773, Adams was 29, Warren 45. The older woman became something of a

British warships crowd Boston Harbor. "We are invaded with fleets," wrote Abigail Adams in 1774, "our commerce not only obstructed but totally ruined."

Although noted British historian Catharine Macaulay (pictured) and Abigail Adams had never met, they enjoyed a lively transatlantic correspondence.

In the early 1770s, impending war with England was the subject of many of Adams and Warren's letters. "The mind is shocked at the thought of shedding human blood, more especially the blood of our countrymen," wrote Adams. But, she added, "such is the present spirit" that Americans would gladly give their lives "with the speech of Cato in their mouths: 'What a pity it is that we can die but once to save our country.'"

Clearly, Abigail Adams was acutely worried about the future. But in June 1774, when her husband was elected to the Continental Congress, she calmly set about packing for his trip to Philadelphia. Writing to him soon after his departure, she said, "I long impatiently to have you upon the stage of action." Meanwhile, concerned about the "storm that was coming on" in Boston, the Adamses had decided that Abigail and the children should leave the city. They moved back to Braintree, where they would remain during the tumultuous years that followed.

Decisions made at the First Continental Congress, as the 1774 meeting came to be known, would profoundly affect the future of the colonies and their inhabitants. Somewhat awed by his new role, John Adams wrote in his diary, "This will be an assembly of the wisest men upon the continent .... I feel myself unequal to this business. A more extensive knowledge of the

role model for Adams, who was deeply impressed with Warren's ability to manage a home and raise children while pursuing her own intellectual interests. Warren, in turn, appreciated Adams's commentary on her literary output. She also enjoyed discussing such daring themes as feminism with her young friend. During the course of their long friendship, Adams and Warren wrote to each other about dozens of subjects that interested them, from political philosophy to public morality to husbands, children, and education.

realm, the colonies, and of commerce as well as of law and policy is necessary than I am master of."

Despite his fears, Adams had no doubts about attending the Congress. "Sink or swim, live or die, survive or perish with my country," he wrote his wife, "is my unalterable determination." He also told her how much he depended on her: "I must entreat you, my dear partner in all the joys and sorrows, prosperity, and adversity of my life, to take a part with me in the struggle."

Now Abigail Adams alone was responsible both for the children and the success of the family farm. From Philadelphia, 300 miles away, John Adams dispatched a stream of letters advising his wife. "I pray for your good health," said one, "[and] entreat you to rouse your whole attention to the family, the stock, the farm, the dairy. Let every article of expense which can possibly be spared be retrenched. Keep the [hired] hands attentive to their business, and [let] the most prudent measures of every kind be adopted and pursued."

John Adams also expressed concern about the education of his children. "Let our ardent anxiety be to mold [their] minds and manners," he urged. Although Charlie and Tommy were still toddlers, Nabby was now nine and Johnny seven. Because Braintree's limited schools had been disrupted by the

Mercy Otis Warren (shown here) successfully combined the roles of wife, mother, and playwright, a feat that inspired Abigail Adams's profound respect.

Delegates take a break during the First Continental Congress, held in Philadelphia in 1774. All 13 colonies except Georgia were represented at the meeting.

political crisis, the children would have to be educated at home. They would need a plan of study, books, tutors. Confident that his wife could handle the job of "school mistress," John Adams outlined a curriculum, which included French, history, philosophy, Latin, and Greek. "If we suffer [the children's] minds to grovel in in-

fancy," he told his wife, "they will grovel all their lives."

To her friend Mercy Warren, Abigail Adams wrote, "I am sensible I have an important trust committed to me, and though I feel myself unequal to it, 'tis still incumbent upon me to discharge it in the best manner I am capable of." Adams, who had always wished she had received a better education herself, was immensely pleased by her husband's conviction that she could educate their children.

Miles apart but as deeply in love as ever, the couple celebrated their 10th wedding anniversary on October 25, 1774. "My much loved friend, I dare not express to you at 300 miles distance how ardently I long for your return," wrote Abigail Adams on the occasion. "Nor dare I describe," she continued, "how earnestly I long to fold to my fluttering heart the dear object of my warmest affections. I feast upon [the idea] with a pleasure known only to those whose hearts and hopes are one." Her husband was less demonstrative, but equally loving. A "delicious" letter from her, he said, was "worth a dozen" of his own.

Regularly arriving in Braintree, his letters contained impressions of Philadelphia ("I shall be killed with kindness in this place"), of the 55 delegates to the Congress ("a collection of the greatest men upon this continent"), and of the work they were doing ("We have had as great questions to discuss as ever engaged the attention of men"). Adams even reported on the meals he was served, which included "the very best of Claret, Madeira, and Burgundy [wine]," and "melons, fine beyond description."

By the time the First Continental Congress adjourned in late October, its members had reached an important decision: All imports from and exports to Britain would be cut off by the following fall unless the Intolerable Acts were repealed by that time. The Congress also issued a Declaration of Rights, which stated that Americans were entitled to the same liberties as those enjoyed by Britons. The delegates agreed to reconvene the following May if their grievances had not been redressed.

Four months after his departure from Boston, John Adams returned to his family in Braintree, to his farm, and to his law practice. Life once again seemed normal, leading even the ever-worried Abigail Adams toward optimism. Writing to Mercy Warren in February 1775, she said, "There really seems to be a ray of light breaking through the palpable darkness which has for so long a time darkened our hemisphere." Soon to come, she said hopefully, were "more favorable scenes and brighter days." But the tranquillity was not to last. A month after Adams's letter, the guns of Lexington and Concord blasted all hope of peace.

Minutemen defend Concord Bridge on April 19, 1775. Poet Ralph Waldo Emerson wrote that "the shot heard round the world" was fired at this battle.

Deeply in love with his wife but fiercely committed to his nation, John Adams faced an ongoing conflict between his personal and public lives.

FIVE

The Road to Independence

After Lexington and Concord there was no turning back: America and Britain were on the road to war. In May 1775 John Adams returned to Philadelphia, where he and the other delegates to the Second Continental Congress would plot the course of the nation's future. In Braintree, Abigail Adams once again assumed total responsibility for her four children and the family farm.

The colonies had not yet decided to seek independence. At this point, their goal was British recognition of their political and civil rights, the repeal of the Intolerable Acts, and an end to taxation without representation in Parliament. No war had been officially declared. Nevertheless, a state closely resembling war was in effect. It was a time of confusion.

It was also a time of tension. Because news could travel no faster than a mounted courier, Adams and her neighbors lived in a state of anxious uncertainty about the events taking place around them. What was that distant rumble? Thunder? Or was it cannon fire? Why were Boston's church bells pealing? Was it true that the British were arresting everyone suspected of participating in the Boston Tea Party?

The air swirled with rumors, but of some events, Abigail Adams was sure. She knew, for example, that Boston was firmly in the hands of the British, and that on May 21 several shiploads of fresh troops had sailed into the harbor. She also knew that on the same day patriots had burned thousands of tons of hay on nearby Grape Island, thus preventing its seizure by the British.

A sizable number of Boston's residents were Tories (British Loyalists) and content to remain in the city under British military rule. Residents who sympathized with the rebel cause, however, were eager to leave. Many of those who managed to escape the city appeared at Abigail Adams's doorstep, hoping for a meal or temporary shelter. She fed and housed as many of these refugees as she could. "We know not what a day will bring forth, nor what distress one hour may throw us into," she said in a letter to her husband.

Dedicated to his country, John Adams knew that his presence in Phil-adelphia was crucial to its future. At the same time, he was consumed with worry about his family. His letters to his wife reflect these dual concerns, mixing news of the congress with domestic questions and advice.

In June 1775, for example, he told her that the congress had selected a general for the fledgling American army. The new commander in chief, said Adams, was "the modest and virtuous, the amiable, generous, and brave George Washington, Esquire." In other letters, Adams gave his wife care-

A young militiaman, preparing to join his unit, bids an emotional farewell to his family. In 1775, Americans found themselves in the midst of an undeclared war.

ful instructions about drying hay, fertilizing the fields, and ridding the fruit trees of caterpillars. "My fancy and wishes and desires," he wrote her, "are at Braintree, among my fields, pastures, and meadows."

Abigail Adams supplied her husband with both domestic news and information about Boston's fast-moving political and military events. He found her letters both personally reassuring and politically useful. She "obliges me," he told one friend, "with clearer and fuller intelligence than I can get from a whole committee of gentlemen." It was from his wife that Adams first heard about the historic British assault on Breed's Hill (usually misidentified as Bunker Hill) on June 17, 1775.

Although Boston was in the hands of the British, American troops surrounded the city on every land side except Charlestown, site of Breed's Hill. When the Americans began to fortify the hill, the British decided to attack. Awakened by the roar of cannon at 3:00 A.M. on June 17, Adams and her son John raced outside to investigate. From the top of a hill on their farm, they saw flashes of fire and thick plumes of smoke above Charlestown. When Adams wrote her husband about the battle, she had not yet learned of its outcome, but she believed that "the day, perhaps the decisive day is come on which the fate of America depends."

A Tory family heads for British-held Boston in 1775. As the war heated up, streams of refugees—both Tory and patriot—became a common sight in Massachusetts.

The Battle of Breed's Hill was not decisive, but it was important. Although the British won the hill, they suffered 1054 casualties to the Americans' 441. It had been, as one British

Addressing Congress in 1775, John Adams proposes that "a gentleman from Virginia"—George Washington—be named commander in chief of the American army.

officer put it, "a dear bought victory"— and it taught the British that defeating the "rude colonials" would be no simple matter. Among the Americans who fell in the battle was Joseph Warren, the 34-year-old doctor who had been one of the Adamses' closest friends. Abigail Adams was grief stricken by the loss. Relaying the sad news to her husband, she wrote, "We mourn for the citizen, the senator, the physician, and the warrior."

Far from the scene of this battle, John Adams was in the thick of another. Gathered in Philadelphia were the colonies' leading citizens, all of them eager to secure a bright future for America. Almost every one of them,

however, held a different idea about that future. Some, like John Adams, his cousin Sam Adams, and Pennsylvania diplomat Benjamin Franklin, believed complete independence from Britain to be the only route. Some favored partial independence; others, a reconciliation with the mother country. The delegates also frequently disagreed about the best way to administer national affairs, and their conversations were not always models of courtesy.

Writing to his wife in July 1775, Adams remarked on "the fidgets, the whims, the caprice, the vanity, the superstition, the irritability" sometimes demonstrated by his colleagues. "When 50 or 60 men," he wrote, "have a country of 1,500 miles extent to fortify, millions to arm and train, a naval power to begin, an extensive commerce to regulate, numerous tribes of Indians to negotiate with, a standing army of 27,000 men to raise, pay, victual [feed], and officer, I really shall pity those 50 or 60 men."

"How difficult the task," responded his sympathetic wife, "to sacrifice ourselves . . . to the public," and "how few have souls capable of so noble an undertaking." Abigail Adams missed her husband enormously, reading and rereading every word he wrote from Philadelphia. She, in turn, had much to tell about her own activities as farmer, teacher, accountant, nurse, and hostess to many of the American military men stationed near Boston. She took special note of one officer she met in the summer of 1775. "I was struck with General Washington," she said. "The gentleman and soldier look agreeably blended in him."

Even during what she called "these calamitous times," Abigail Adams demonstrated extraordinary vitality and optimism, impressing her associates and even surprising herself. In a letter

Fortifying Breed's Hill, American militiamen work through the dark night. At 3:00 A.M. on June 17, 1775, the British attacked.

General Joseph Warren lies mortally wounded after the Battle of Breed's Hill. Abigail Adams was deeply grieved by the death of the young physician.

to Mercy Warren, she said she feared that only "a degree of stupidity or insensibility" would allow her to "feel so tranquil amidst such scenes." Yet, she said, "I cannot charge myself with an unfeeling heart." Perhaps, she decided, her good spirits were due simply to the absence of a "restless, anxious disposition."

Adams's "feeling heart" was to be severely tested. Her husband came home for a vacation in August, but he could stay only three weeks. "I am obliged to summon all my patriotism to feel willing to part with him again," she told Warren. "You will readily believe me when I say that I make no small sacrifice to the public." Soon

after John Adams returned to Philadelphia, the Boston area was swept by dysentery, an often fatal intestinal disease. It struck hard in Abigail Adams's household.

First to die were her brother-in-law, Elihu Adams, and his infant daughter. Next came the Adams's housemaid, Patty. When Adams and her son Thomas became ill, her mother nursed them back to health, then caught the disease herself. Elizabeth Smith died in her daughter's arms on October 1. "How can I tell you (O, my bursting heart)," wrote Abigail Adams to her husband, "that my dear mother has left me?" Although Adams said she was unsure she could bear "this severe and heavy stroke," she gradually regained both her strength and her positive outlook. "Heaven," she prayed, "make me properly thankful that it is not my sad lot to mourn the loss of a husband."

Meanwhile, John Adams and his fellow delegates continued their fierce debate over America's future. Radicals—whose number included both Abigail and John Adams—continued to favor total independence; conservatives still hoped for a reconciliation with England. In early 1776, however, the tide suddenly turned toward the radicals. Largely responsible was a small pamphlet published by a recent British immigrant named Thomas Paine.

COMMON SENSE;

ADDRESSED TO THE

INHABITANTS

OF

AMERICA,

On the following interesting

SUBJECTS.

I. Of the Origin and Design of Government in general, with concise Remarks on the English Constitution.

II. Of Monarchy and Hereditary Succession.

III. Thoughts on the present State of American Affairs.

IV. Of the present Ability of America, with some miscellaneous Reflections.

Man knows no Master save creating HEAVEN,
Or those whom choice and common good ordain.

THOMSON.

PHILADELPHIA;

Printed, and Sold, by R. BELL, in Third-Street.

MDCCLXXVI.

Common Sense, *written by Thomas Paine (inset), delivered a powerful argument for American independence. The incendiary pamphlet appeared in 1776.*

Paine's *Common Sense*, an impassioned plea for American independence, was political dynamite. The very idea, Paine asserted, that "a continent can be perpetually governed by an island" was absurd. The monarchy of George III was brutal and corrupt, with no more right to rule America than a satellite had to rule the sun. "Ye that dare oppose not only the tyranny but the tyrant," thundered Paine, "stand forth!"

Reprinted many times, *Common Sense* was passed from hand to hand and eventually read by thousands of Americans. Although not all its readers were converted to Paine's arguments, his fiery tract had a powerful influence on many. One of them was the hitherto conservative George Washington, who

Threatened by Washington's surprise takeover of Dorchester Heights, General William Howe (center) leads his forces out of Boston on March 17, 1776.

called Paine's work "sound doctrine and unanswerable reasoning." John Adams, too, approved of it. He sent his wife a copy, calling it a "vindication" of their own beliefs. She agreed. "I am charmed with the sentiments of *Common Sense*," she wrote, "and wonder how an honest heart . . . can hesitate one moment at adopting them."

Six months would pass before America adopted the ideas of Paine, the Adamses, and other radicals. In the meantime, the cannon continued to roar. In February, patriot militia defeated a major uprising of Loyalists in North Carolina, thereby preventing a British invasion of the South. Far to the north, American troops under General Benedict Arnold made a bloody but unsuccessful attempt to capture the Canadian city of Quebec. Then, in March, George Washington managed to fortify the steep hills of the Dorchester Peninsula, overlooking Boston.

Washington's move took the British by surprise. General William Howe, now commanding British forces in Boston, had no desire to remain in the direct range of Washington's guns. He sent a message to the American general, offering him the city in return for the safe evacuation of his army. Washington agreed. On March 17, Howe dumped his cannon into the harbor, loaded his men aboard British warships, and set sail for British-held Canada. Looking on as the hated occupying forces departed the city was Abigail Adams.

From the hill on their farm, she told her husband, she had "a view of the largest fleet ever seen in America. You may count upwards of 170 sail. They look like a forest. . . . Our general may say with Caesar, 'Veni, vidi, vici [I came, I saw, I conquered].' "

Like the rest of the Massachusetts patriots, Adams was immensely relieved to see the last of the British, at least for the moment. Under British rule, she recalled in a letter to her husband, "We knew not . . . whether we could plant or sow with safety; whether, when we had toiled, we could reap the fruits of our own industry; whether we could rest in our own cottages; or whether we should not be driven from the seacoasts to seek shelter in the wilderness."

With the immediate threat of British hostility relaxed, Abigail Adams's thoughts returned to America's separation from England. "I long to hear that you have declared an independency," she wrote her husband on March 31, 1776. "And by the way," she added, "in the new code of laws, which I suppose it will be necessary for you to make, I desire you would remember the ladies, and be more generous and favorable to them than your ancestors."

Warming to her subject, she continued, "Do not put such unlimited power into the hands of the husbands. Remember, all men would be tyrants if they could. If particular care and attention is not paid to the ladies, we are determined to foment a rebellion, and will not hold ourselves bound by any laws in which we have no voice or representation."

In the two centuries since Adams wrote these words, historians have

"And by the way," begins a celebrated passage in this 1776 letter from Abigail Adams to her husband, "I desire you would remember the ladies...."

debated her intent. Some believe she was only half-serious; in 18th-century America, the idea of women having a "voice"—or a vote—would have shocked almost everyone, even such independent-minded men and women as Abigail and John Adams. Others maintain that Adams sincerely hoped to persuade her husband to change America's English-based laws, under which women had virtually no legal rights. In any case, John Adams's response to his wife's letter was written in a humorous tone.

"We have been told that our struggle has loosened the bonds of government everywhere," he said. "That children and apprentices were disobedient—that schools and colleges were grown turbulent—that Indians slighted their guardians and Negroes grew insolent to their masters. But your letter was the first intimation that another tribe, more numerous and powerful than all the rest, were grown discontented."

His wife, said John Adams, had overstated her case. "We have only the name of masters," he insisted "and rather than give up this, which would completely subject us to the despotism of the petticoat, I hope General Washington and all our brave heroes would fight."

Abigail Adams was probably amused by her husband's response, but she wrote back in mock-fury: "I cannot say that I think you very generous to the ladies, for while you are proclaiming

Conferring on the Declaration of Independence are Benjamin Franklin (left), Thomas Jefferson (holding manuscript), and John Adams (second from right).

peace and good will to men, emancipating all nations, you insist upon retaining an absolute power over wives."

Drawing a subtle comparison between the male-female argument and America's quarrel with England, she added, "But you must remember that arbitrary power is, like most other things which are very hard, very liable to be broken.... We have it in our power not only to free ourselves but to subdue our masters, and without violence, throw both your natural and legal authority at your feet."

Less than two months after these affectionate opponents had exchanged sallies about independence, the Congress passed a declaration whose ringing words changed history forever: "We, therefore, the Representatives of the UNITED STATES OF AMERICA, in General Congress ... solemnly Publish and Declare, That these United Colonies are, and of right ought to be, free and independent states...."

IN CONGRESS, JULY 4, 1776.

The unanimous Declaration of the thirteen united States of America,

When in the Course of human events, it becomes necessary for one people to dissolve the political bands which have connected them with another, and to assume among the powers of the earth, the separate and equal station to which the Laws of Nature and of Nature's God entitle them, a decent respect to the opinions of mankind requires that they should declare the causes which impel them to the separation. — We hold these truths to be self-evident, that all men are created equal, that they are endowed by their Creator with certain unalienable Rights, that among these are Life, Liberty and the pursuit of Happiness. — That to secure these rights, Governments are instituted among Men, deriving their just powers from the consent of the governed, — That whenever any Form of Government becomes destructive of these ends, it is the Right of the People to alter or to abolish it, and to institute new Government, laying its foundation on such principles and organizing its powers in such form, as to them shall seem most likely to effect their Safety and Happiness. Prudence, indeed, will dictate that Governments long established should not be changed for light and transient causes; and accordingly all experience hath shewn, that mankind are more disposed to suffer, while evils are sufferable, than to right themselves by abolishing the forms to which they are accustomed. But when a long train of abuses and usurpations, pursuing invariably the same Object evinces a design to reduce them under absolute Despotism, it is their right, it is their duty, to throw off such Government, and to provide new Guards for their future security. — Such has been the patient sufferance of these Colonies; and such is now the necessity which constrains them to alter their former Systems of Government. The history of the present King of Great Britain is a history of repeated injuries and usurpations, all having in direct object the establishment of an absolute Tyranny over these States. To prove this, let Facts be submitted to a candid world. — He has refused his Assent to Laws, the most wholesome and necessary for the public good. — He has forbidden his Governors to pass Laws of immediate and pressing importance, unless suspended in their operation till his Assent should be obtained; and when so suspended, he has utterly neglected to attend to them. — He has refused to pass other Laws for the accommodation of large districts of people, unless those people would relinquish the right of Representation in the Legislature, a right inestimable to them and formidable to tyrants only. — He has called together legislative bodies at places unusual, uncomfortable, and distant from the depository of their public Records, for the sole purpose of fatiguing them into compliance with his measures. — He has dissolved Representative Houses repeatedly, for opposing with manly firmness his invasions on the rights of the people. — He has refused for a long time, after such dissolutions, to cause others to be elected; whereby the Legislative powers, incapable of Annihilation, have returned to the People at large for their exercise; the State remaining in the mean time exposed to all the dangers of invasion from without, and convulsions within. — He has endeavoured to prevent the population of these States; for that purpose obstructing the Laws for Naturalization of Foreigners; refusing to pass others to encourage their migrations hither, and raising the conditions of new Appropriations of Lands. — He has obstructed the Administration of Justice, by refusing his Assent to Laws for establishing Judiciary powers. — He has made Judges dependent on his Will alone, for the tenure of their offices, and the amount and payment of their salaries. — He has erected a multitude of New Offices, and sent hither swarms of Officers to harrass our people, and eat out their substance. — He has kept among us, in times of peace, Standing Armies without the Consent of our legislatures. — He has affected to render the Military independent of and superior to the Civil power. — He has combined with others to subject us to a jurisdiction foreign to our constitution, and unacknowledged by our laws; giving his Assent to their Acts of pretended Legislation: — For Quartering large bodies of armed troops among us: — For protecting them, by a mock Trial, from punishment for any Murders which they should commit on the Inhabitants of these States: — For cutting off our Trade with all parts of the world: — For imposing Taxes on us without our Consent: — For depriving us in many cases, of the benefits of Trial by Jury: — For transporting us beyond Seas to be tried for pretended offences: — For abolishing the free System of English Laws in a neighbouring Province, establishing therein an Arbitrary government, and enlarging its Boundaries so as to render it at once an example and fit instrument for introducing the same absolute rule into these Colonies: — For taking away our Charters, abolishing our most valuable Laws, and altering fundamentally the Forms of our Governments: — For suspending our own Legislatures, and declaring themselves invested with power to legislate for us in all cases whatsoever. — He has abdicated Government here, by declaring us out of his Protection and waging War against us. — He has plundered our seas, ravaged our Coasts, burnt our towns, and destroyed the lives of our people. — He is at this time transporting large Armies of foreign Mercenaries to compleat the works of death, desolation and tyranny, already begun with circumstances of Cruelty & perfidy scarcely paralleled in the most barbarous ages, and totally unworthy the Head of a civilized nation. — He has constrained our fellow Citizens taken Captive on the high Seas to bear Arms against their Country, to become the executioners of their friends and Brethren, or to fall themselves by their Hands. — He has excited domestic insurrections amongst us, and has endeavoured to bring on the inhabitants of our frontiers, the merciless Indian Savages, whose known rule of warfare, is an undistinguished destruction of all ages, sexes and conditions. In every stage of these Oppressions We have Petitioned for Redress in the most humble terms: Our repeated Petitions have been answered only by repeated injury. A Prince, whose character is thus marked by every act which may define a Tyrant, is unfit to be the ruler of a free people. Nor have We been wanting in attentions to our Brittish brethren. We have warned them from time to time of attempts by their legislature to extend an unwarrantable jurisdiction over us. We have reminded them of the circumstances of our emigration and settlement here. We have appealed to their native justice and magnanimity, and we have conjured them by the ties of our common kindred to disavow these usurpations, which, would inevitably interrupt our connections and correspondence. They too have been deaf to the voice of justice and of consanguinity. We must, therefore, acquiesce in the necessity, which denounces our Separation, and hold them, as we hold the rest of mankind, Enemies in War, in Peace Friends. —

We, therefore, the Representatives of the united States of America, in General Congress, Assembled, appealing to the Supreme Judge of the world for the rectitude of our intentions, do, in the Name, and by Authority of the good People of these Colonies, solemnly publish and declare, That these United Colonies are, and of Right ought to be Free and Independent States; that they are Absolved from all Allegiance to the British Crown, and that all political connection between them and the State of Great Britain, is and ought to be totally dissolved; and that as Free and Independent States, they have full Power to levy War, conclude Peace, contract Alliances, establish Commerce, and to do all other Acts and Things which Independent States may of right do. — And for the support of this Declaration, with a firm reliance on the protection of divine Providence, we mutually pledge to each other our Lives, our Fortunes and our sacred Honor.

Button Gwinnett
Lyman Hall
Geo Walton.
Wm Hooper
Joseph Hewes,
John Penn
Edward Rutledge 1.
Thos Heyward Junr.
Thomas Lynch Junr.
Arthur Middleton
John Hancock
Samuel Chase
Wm. Paca
Thos. Stone
Charles Carroll of Carrollton
George Wythe
Richard Henry Lee
Th Jefferson
Benja. Harrison
Thos Nelson jr.
Francis Lightfoot Lee
Carter Braxton
Robt Morris
Benjamin Rush
Benja. Franklin
John Morton
Geo Clymer
Jas. Smith
Geo. Taylor
James Wilson
Geo. Ross
Caesar Rodney
Geo Read
Tho M:Kean
Wm Floyd
Phil. Livingston
Frans. Lewis
Lewis Morris
Richd. Stockton
Jno Witherspoon
Fras. Hopkinson
John Hart
Abra Clark
Josiah Bartlett
Wm. Whipple
Saml Adams
John Adams
Robt Treat Paine
Elbridge Gerry
Step. Hopkins
William Ellery
Roger Sherman
Sam. el Huntington
Wm. Williams
Oliver Wolcott
Matthew Thornton

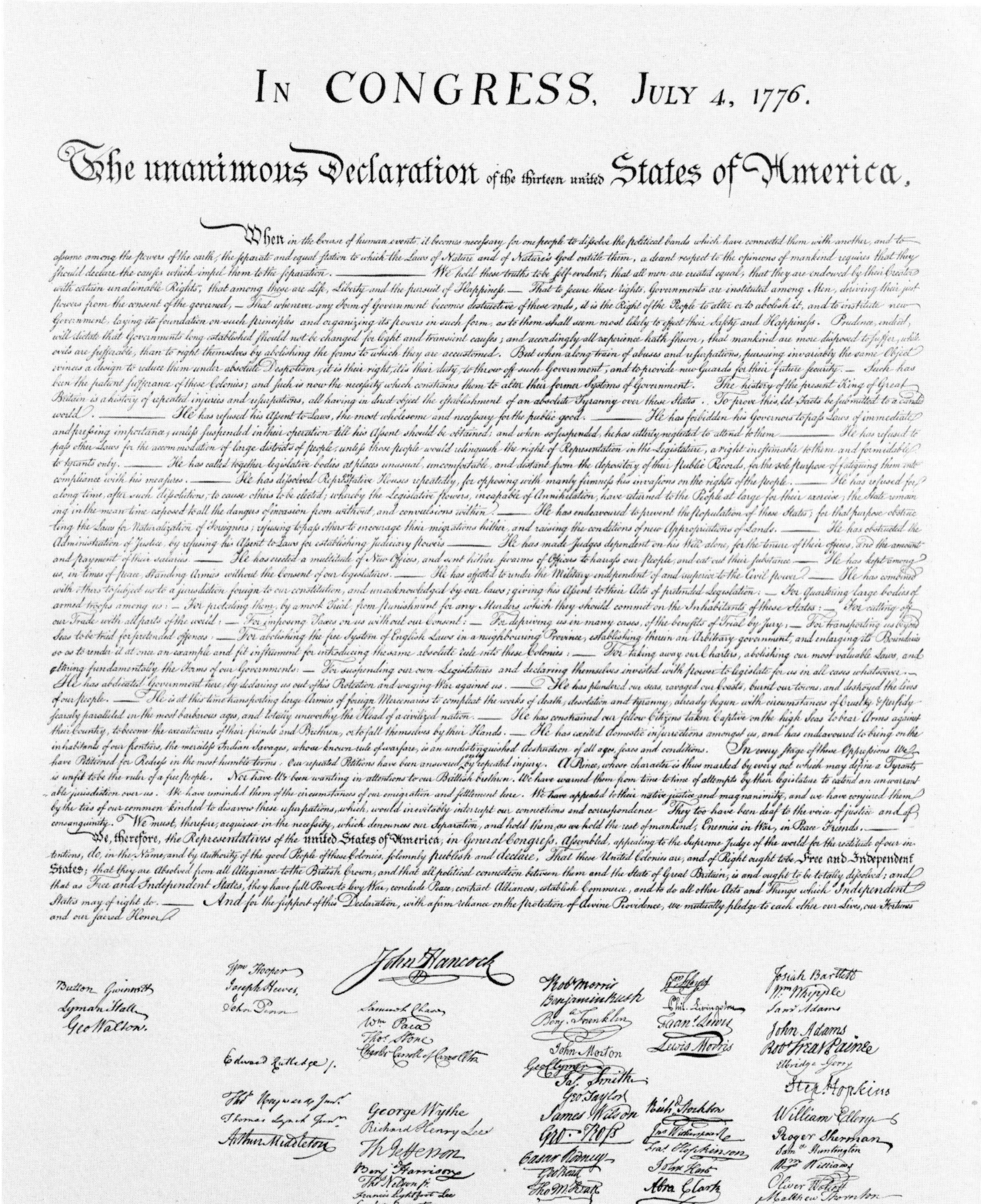

Completed on July 4, 1776, the Declaration of Independence stunned the world. The signature of John Adams appears at right, fourth from the top.

SIX

"Give Me the Man I Love!"

Elated by the signing of the Declaration of Independence, John Adams told his wife that the Fourth of July "ought to be solemnized with pomp and parade, with shows, games, sports, guns, bells, bonfires, and illuminations from one end of this continent to the other from this time forward forever more." On a more somber note, he added, "I am well aware of the toil and blood and treasure that it will cost us to maintain this declaration and support and defend these states."

Abigail Adams was as enthusiastic about the signing of the declaration as her husband. She told him she was proud "that a person so nearly connected with me has had the honor of being a principal actor" in this national drama. "May the foundation of our new constitution," she said, "be justice, truth, and righteousness." When the Declaration of Independence was publicly read in Boston, "the bells rang . . . and every face appeared joyful," she reported. "Thus endeth royal authority in this state, and all the people shall say amen," she concluded with satisfaction.

Adams's excitement about the long-awaited declaration was tempered with worry about her family's health. Fearing an outbreak of smallpox, she had brought her children to Boston to be inoculated against the deadly disease. Inoculation was a dangerous procedure in the 18th century. After being exposed to a mild form of the disease, a patient was usually immune to further attacks, but some patients contracted severe cases of smallpox, which could end in disfigurement or death. Abigail, Nabby, John Quincy, and Thomas were successfully immunized, but four-year-old Charles caught the disease.

A Philadelphia crowd cheers the Declaration of Independence. After the document was read in Boston, reported Abigail Adams, "every face appeared joyful."

Fired with rage against the British, New Yorkers topple a statue of George III. The bronze likeness was later melted down and made into American bullets.

John Adams was horrified to learn about the illness of his "pathetic little hero, Charles." He told his wife that her letter had "fixed an arrow in my heart, which will not be drawn out until the next post appears, and then, perhaps, instead of being withdrawn, it will be driven deeper." After several frightening weeks, the young patient recovered. His worried father was flooded with relief. "I feel quite light," John Adams wrote his wife. "I did not know what fast hold that little prattler Charles had upon me before."

Awaiting Charles's full recovery, Abigail Adams stayed in a "pretty closet" (bedroom) in her aunt's house in Boston. From here she wrote her husband, "I do not covet my neighbors' goods, but . . . I always had a fancy for a closet with a window which I could more peculiarly call my own." Poring over her husband's letters and looking forward to his next trip home, she said, "I have spent the three days past almost entirely with you. . . . I have amused myself in reading and thinking of my absent friend [as she called her husband], sometimes with a mixture of pain, sometimes with pleasure, sometimes anticipating a joyful and happy meeting. . . . I have held you to my bosom till my whole soul has dissolved in tenderness and my pen fallen from my hand." Her husband, she hoped, would not find her feelings "inconsistent with the stern value of a senator and a patriot."

When John Adams returned to Braintree in October 1776, he expected to stay for good. The Massachusetts legislature, however, once again named him as a delegate to the Continental Congress, and after much discussion with his wife, he decided to go back to Philadelphia in January. Pregnant again, Abigail Adams found it harder than ever to part with her husband. "I had it in my heart to dissuade him from going, and I know I should have prevailed," she wrote Mercy Warren, "but our public affairs at that time wore so gloomy an aspect that I thought that if ever his assistance was wanted, it must be at such a time. I therefore resigned myself to suffer much anxiety and many melancholy hours for this year to come."

Public affairs were indeed "gloomy." Soon after the Declaration of Independence was published, George Washington marched his troops to New York, where he expected the next British offensive. Meeting his 19,000-man army were 32,000 seasoned British troops and hundreds of warships under the command of General William Howe. Washington, overwhelmed by superior forces, retreated to New Jersey, then crossed the Delaware River to Pennsylvania. The American Revolution had reached a discouraging stalemate.

Abigail Adams's worries, however, were concentrated on her own affairs. Once again solely responsible for her

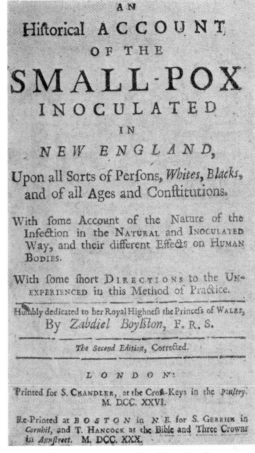

An 18th-century medical book discusses inoculation against smallpox, the era's most dreaded disease. Abigail Adams had all her children inoculated.

children and the farm, she was faced with soaring prices, shortages of household goods and farm labor, and rumors of a new British attack on Boston. Still, she managed to feed her family, weave cloth, pay the bills, and oversee the tending of her crops and livestock. "What cannot be helped must be endured," she said firmly. She was comforted by thoughts of her expected baby, which both she and her husband hoped would be a girl.

In July 1777 she delivered a stillborn daughter. "It appeared to be a very fine babe," she told her husband sadly, "and as it never opened its eyes in this world it looked as though they were only closed for sleep." Offering what comfort she could, she added, "We ought patiently to submit to the dispensation of heaven." John Adams was heartbroken by the news. "Is it not unaccountable that one should feel so strong an affection for an infant that one has never seen nor shall see?" he wrote. "Yet I must confess to you, the loss of this sweet little girl has most tenderly and sensibly affected me."

Meanwhile, the nation was buzzing with rumors about the next moves of Howe and the British fleet. Everyone knew they had sailed out of New York, but where were they headed? Some said Rhode Island, some said Boston. Others insisted Howe's destination

George Washington crosses the Delaware in late 1776. His attack on the British at Trenton, New Jersey, resulted in one of the winter's few American victories.

Outnumbered and outgunned, American troops lose the Battle of Brandywine Creek on September 11, 1777. Two weeks later, the British took Philadelphia.

was Philadelphia, a possibility that alarmed Abigail Adams. "Don't be anxious for my safety," wrote her husband. "If Howe comes here, I shall run away, I suppose, with the rest."

Then, sounding far more warlike than usual, John Adams said, "I confess I feel myself so much injured by these barbarian Britons that I have a strong inclination to meet them in the field.... It is too late a period in the war for me to think of girding on a sword, but if I had the last four years to run over again, I certainly would."

Those who had predicted a British invasion of Philadelphia proved cor-rect. Brushing Washington's army aside at the Battle of Brandywine Creek, Howe entered Philadelphia in September 1777. Washington retired to winter quarters at Valley Forge and the Continental Congress retreated to York, Pennsylvania. From this tempo-rary capital, Adams wrote a soothing letter to his wife. "I am very comfort-ably situated here," he said. "My health is as good as common, and, I assure you, my spirits not the worse for the loss of Philadelphia."

The following month the war reached a major turning point: After losing a series of battles in New York

General Benedict Arnold (on horseback) is temporarily stopped at the Battle of Saratoga in 1777. Recovering, he helped defeat General John Burgoyne's British army.

State, British general John Burgoyne ordered his 5,000 men to lay down their arms at Saratoga. The American victory amazed European observers, particularly the French, Britain's traditional enemies. France, ruled by King Louis XVI, was vitally interested in the fate of the American revolutionaries, to whom it had been supplying substantial financial aid. England would be seriously weakened by the loss of its American colonies; France, in turn, would be strengthened.

Writing to her husband after "the joyful news" of Burgoyne's surrender, Abigail Adams noted that "this day"— it was October 25, 1777—"completes 13 years since we were solemnly united in wedlock; 3 years of the time we have been cruelly separated. I have patiently as I could endured it with the belief that you were serving your country." At this point, Adams was looking forward to an extended reunion with her husband, who had been granted a leave of absence from the Continental Congress and who was due home in late November. She had no idea that greater demands than ever were about to be made on her "patient endurance."

John Adams resumed his law practice as soon as he arrived in Braintree. Three weeks later, he learned that the Congress had appointed him to represent the United States in France. He was to depart as soon as possible for Paris, where he would join Benjamin Franklin in negotiating a U.S. alliance with France.

Abigail Adams was staggered by the appointment. The trip to France, 3,000 miles away, would be filled with danger, both from the stormy Atlantic and from the British navy. Letters would take many weeks to cross the ocean, and the assignment might take months, even years. "Must I cheerfully comply with the demands of my country?" she asked a friend. "Can I ... consent to be separated from him whom my heart esteems above all earthly things, and for an unlimited time?" But she knew the answer. Her husband could not refuse to serve his country, and she could not refuse to let him go.

On a cold, windy day in February 1778, John Adams sailed for France aboard the 24-gun frigate *Boston*. With him was his 10-year-old son, John Quincy. Abigail Adams believed the journey would be good for the boy, who would serve as his father's clerk and, at the same time, learn French and see the world. Nevertheless, she was desolated by the parting. "Cannot you imagine me seated by my fireside," she wrote a friend, "bereft of my better half, and added to that, a limb lopped off to heighten the anguish?"

John Adams and his son arrived in Paris in mid-April, but their first letters home did not reach Braintree until the end of June, more than four months after they left. Thus began one of the most difficult periods of Abigail Adams's life. She was desperately worried about her husband and son, concerned about lack of progress in the war, short of money, anxious about the education of her three younger children, and distressed about running the farm single-handedly.

Adams was not a woman to sit and brood, and she did what she could to improve her circumstances. She leased the farm, correctly judging that renting

Encamped at Valley Forge in 1777, George Washington (in cape) confers with the marquis de Lafayette, one of several French officers in his army.

it would be more profitable than operating it herself, and she sent 12-year-old Nabby to school in Boston. Charles and Thomas, now respectively eight and six, were not old enough to go to school, so she tutored them herself. Still, time passed slowly, and she agonized about the lack of mail from her husband.

Frantically busy in Paris, Adams did not write as often as he had from Philadelphia, and many of the letters he did write were lost at sea. But even those that reached Braintree failed to make his wife happy. Afraid that his correspondence would fall into British hands, he wrote in a cool, formal style. The tone of these letters resulted in the first angry words Abigail and John Adams had ever exchanged in writing.

"By heaven, if you could, you have changed hearts with some frozen Laplander, or made a voyage to a region that has chilled every drop of your blood," exclaimed Abigail Adams at one point. "The affection I feel for my friend is of the tenderest kind," she added. "Angels can witness to its purity—what care I then for the ridicule of Britain should this testimony of it fall into their hands?" Stung by his wife's uncharacteristically harsh words, John Adams replied, "Can protestations of affection be necessary? Can tokens of remembrance be desired? The very idea of this sickens me. Am I not wretched enough in this banishment without this? I beg you

France's Louis XVI (above) favored America in its struggle against England, his nation's longtime foe. He lent millions of dollars to the revolutionaries.

would nevermore write to me in such a strain, for it really makes me unhappy."

In other letters, however, the Adamses resumed their familiar exchange of information. Mail from Abigail brought news of the children and of the French and American officials who often called on her. Mail from John carried glowing descriptions of French architecture, customs, art, and people. "To tell the truth," said Adams to his wife, "I admire the ladies here. Don't be jealous. They are handsome and very well educated."

Abigail Adams was not jealous; she was delighted. "I can hear of the brilliant accomplishments of any of my sex with pleasure, and rejoice in that liberality of sentiment which acknowledges them," she said. "At the same time," she added, reverting to one of her pet subjects, "I regret the trifling, narrow, contracted education of the females of my own country.... You need not be told how much female education is neglected, nor how fashionable it has been to ridicule female learning."

In early 1779, John Adams decided to head home, leaving the French negotiations in Benjamin Franklin's capable hands. After spending months looking for a westbound ship, he and his son finally boarded a French frigate in mid-June. Because of lost and delayed mail, Abigail Adams knew nothing of her husband's plans. When he and John Quincy appeared on her doorstep in August, she was overcome with happiness, instantly forgetting all complaints about her husband's unaffectionate letters.

The major action of the war was now centered in the South, and New England was calm. Abigail and John Adams spent the sunny days of the late fall much as they had during the early days of their marriage: walking in the woods, checking on their fields and vegetable gardens, visiting friends and relatives. This time of tranquillity lasted for only three months. In Octo-

From a hill on her farm, Abigail Adams could see both the village of Braintree and the Atlantic Ocean (upper left), which divided her from her beloved husband.

ber, the Continental Congress gave John Adams a new assignment: As America's representative, he was to leave at once for France. He would remain there until the British were ready to end the war, and then he would negotiate a peace treaty.

Abigail Adams never got used to her husband's absences. Each departure, it seemed, was more painful than the last. But she knew he felt deeply honored by his new responsibility, and she made no effort to keep him at home. The couple decided that on this journey, he would have the company of both John Quincy and nine-year-old Charles. The boys, thought Abigail Adams, needed to spend more time with their father; furthermore, a trip to Europe would be more educational than years of schooling at home. The three Adams males set sail for France in mid-November.

Abigail Adams and her husband loved each other wholeheartedly; why, then, did they agree to live apart for such long periods? "There is absolutely no doubt that these separations made both of them miserable," writes Adams biographer Lynne Withey. In her 1981 book, *Dearest Friend*, Withey suggests that the Adamses "believed that they endured their personal misery for the sake of their country's cause, that their own happiness was less important than the public good."

John Adams was a highly respected public figure, and, says Withey, "his wife basked in [his] glory . . . . He shared the details of his work with her and sought her advice. She relished this involvement, for she was as fascinated with politics as he." Withey points out that Abigail Adams understood her husband's "need for political involvement and recognition, and could not bring herself to stand in his way." Although she could have persuaded him to stay home, she knew he would be unhappy if he did. "Miserable when he was gone, she would have been equally miserable if he had stayed unwillingly and lived out a life of thwarted ambition."

Adams used her latest period of "widowhood," as she called it, to expand her horizons. Managing the family's finances—traditionally the husband's job—became second nature to her, and she began to enjoy it. She grew skilled at financial trading, exchanging hard currency (silver) for the paper money issued by the Continental Congress, which rose and fell in value. She also became a modestly successful merchant, ordering cloth, rugs, china dishes, and glassware from Holland and Spain and reselling them at a profit to eager customers in Braintree. Making use of her newly discovered financial skills, she kept an eye out for farmland, acquiring several small neighboring farms when they were offered at attractive prices.

Keeping in touch with her husband's political associates, Adams stayed as well-informed about current events as any man in the country. Given the customs of the day, when women could not vote, were not encouraged to speak on public issues, could not own property if they were married, and were denied the option of pursuing careers if they were single, Adams's activities were remarkable. Still, she thought of herself as an extension of the man she married. "For myself," she once said, "I have little ambition or pride—for my husband, I freely own I have much."

Six months after John Adams and his sons left for France, the United States suffered its worst defeat of the war: On May 12, 1780, American forces surrendered Charleston, South Carolina, to an overwhelming British force.

Sophisticated Parisiennes exchange quips with their admirers. Adams was pleased when her husband praised the "handsome and well-educated" women of France.

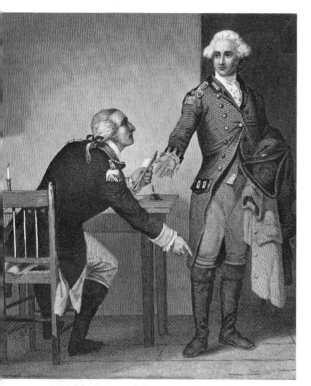

Benedict Arnold passes American military secrets to a British spy in 1780. His action shocked his countrymen and made his name a permanent synonym for "traitor."

Moving quickly across South Carolina, British forces under General Charles Cornwallis won one battle after another, putting most of the state under the British flag. Then, in September, shocked Americans learned that one of their own military heroes, General Benedict Arnold, had turned traitor, selling military secrets to the enemy. These were dark days for the young republic.

"Our present situation is very disagreeable," wrote Abigail Adams to her husband. Still, she remained optimistic. In the past, she said, "When our enemies have supposed us to be subdued, we have risen the conquerors. That Charleston is taken is a truth—yet ... each one is reanimated with spirit to remedy the evil."

The nation's spirit was indeed rising. By the summer of 1781, Washington had managed to trap the bulk of the British army at its own base in Yorktown, Virginia. Aided by French troops and battleships, Washington's army attacked the British on October 9. Eight days later, General Cornwallis raised the white flag of surrender. The Battle of Yorktown was not the last military action of the Revolution, but it clearly signaled the defeat of the British. George III was now ready to negotiate for peace.

Like her compatriots, Abigail Adams rejoiced over Washington's stunning Yorktown victory. "America may boast that she has accomplished what no power before her ever did [when] contending with Britain," she exulted. Then, as usual, she considered the news in terms of her husband. "This event, while it must fill Britain with despondency," she wrote him, "must render a negotiation [for peace] easier and more advantageous to America."

Peace negotiations, however, proved far from easy. In return for substantial

French assistance, America had promised it would sign no peace treaty without French agreement. Cooperation between the two nations was, therefore, crucial. But France's foreign minister, the suave and elegant Count Charles de Vergennes, had little use for blustery and blunt-spoken John Adams. Hoping to offset Adams's authority, Vergennes persuaded the American Congress to replace the Braintree lawyer with a whole delegation, which included diplomats Benjamin Franklin and John Jay.

The Americans found themselves entangled in seemingly endless wrangling with both their former enemies, the British, and their current allies, the French. John Adams called it "a constant scuffle, morning, noon, and night." Not until September 1783 was a treaty signed and the war formally ended. In the two years that elapsed between Yorktown and the peace treaty, John Adams and his wife conducted a lengthy written debate about their future. Should he come home, leaving the negotiations to Franklin

George Washington inspects British troops after their 1781 surrender at Yorktown, Virginia. French assistance helped make the American victory possible.

and Jay? Or should she join him in Europe?

Whatever they decided, they knew they had to be together. "Hope and fear have been the two ruling passions of . . . my life, and I have been bandied from one to the other like a tennis ball," wrote Abigail Adams. "Life is too short to have the dearest of its enjoyments curtailed. . . . Give me the man I love!" From Paris, John Adams wrote, "I must go to you or you must come to me. I cannot live in this horrid solitude."

In September 1783, soon after the peace treaty was signed, Adams, Jay, and Franklin received instructions from Congress to open negotiations for commercial treaties between the United States and as many European

As ambassadors (left to right) Franklin, Jay, and Adams look on, their British counterpart signs the 1783 Paris Treaty, officially ending the American Revolution.

and African nations as possible. This assignment would mean spending even more time abroad, and Adams finally made up his mind: He wrote to his wife and asked her to join him as soon as possible. Vastly relieved that the uncertainty was over and yearning to see her husband, she sent Thomas and Charles (who had returned from Europe in early 1782) to live with her sister, arranged for an uncle to look after the farm, and booked passage for herself and Nabby on the *Active*, an American merchant ship scheduled to leave Boston in June 1784.

When he realized his wife was really coming, John Adams was jubilant. Talking to a newly married colleague in Paris, he said, "I hope to be married once more myself, in a few months, to a very amiable lady whom I have inhumanely left a widow in America for nine years, with the exception of a few weeks only." That lady's consent to his long absence, he said, gave her "good title to the character of a heroine."

Nabby Adams sat for this portrait by Mather Brown in 1785. At 19, said Abigail Adams, her daughter displayed "a prudence and steadiness beyond her years."

SEVEN

European Sojourn

On July 20, 1784, exactly one month after they left Boston, Abigail Adams and her daughter landed in England. Because unpredictable winds and weather made it impossible to pinpoint exact arrival dates for sailing ships, John Adams had waited in France for word of their appearance. When he got it, he was "the happiest man on earth," and "20 years younger than I was yesterday." He told his wife to buy whatever clothing she needed, "let the expense be what it may," and said he would be at her side within a week.

The Adams women had barely settled into their London hotel when they received a caller: a tall, handsome young man dressed in the height of fashion. Not until he opened his arms and said, "O, my mama and my dear sister!" was Abigail Adams sure that this elegant man of the world was her 17-year-old son, John Quincy. But no matter how much he had matured, she wrote her sister Mary Cranch, he was still "the same good-humored lad he formerly was."

Her next visitor was that "best of husbands and friends," John Adams himself. He looked a little older and somewhat heavier, but to Abigail and Nabby Adams he was a beautiful sight. The reunion of the four Adamses was joyful. Writing about it to Cranch, Abigail Adams said, "Poets and painters wisely draw a veil over those scenes which surpass the pen of the one and the pencil of the other; we were indeed a very happy family once more."

The day after John Adams arrived in London, he took his family to Paris, where he was in the midst of complex trade negotiations. Arriving in the French capital in mid-August, they moved at once to an imposing stone mansion in suburban Auteuil. The house was four miles from the center of Paris, but it was close to Benjamin Franklin's residence, where Adams and the other trade commissioners held their meetings.

Massachusetts-bred Abigail Adams was alternately intrigued and scandalized by France, its people, and its customs. Like any other tourist, she was awestruck by Paris's magnificent Notre Dame Cathedral, charmed by the exquisite gardens of the Tuileries, and enchanted by the romantic, tree-shaded paths of the Bois de Boulogne. But she was appalled by Paris's open sewers and garbage-strewn streets. "The city," she said, "is the very dirtiest place I ever saw."

She was also shocked by the casual way Frenchwomen bestowed their kisses—one on each cheek of almost

The Adams's residence in France, a large and stately mansion just outside Paris, was a far cry from their simple house in Braintree.

everyone they met, including men! Even more scandalous to the puritanical New Englander was the French habit of making every Sunday a holiday. To Adams, the Sabbath was a somber day on which to attend church and read sermons, not a time to sing and dance or picnic in the park. Writing to a friend at home, she sniffed, "If you ask me what is the business of life here, I answer pleasure."

Not even the starchy Adams, however, could resist all the pleasures of Paris. Here, at the age of 39, she attended her first opera and found it thrilling. "O! The music, vocal and instrumental, it has a soft persuasive power," she wrote Mary Cranch. She eventually learned to admire ballet, but she was highly disconcerted by her first view of it. "Girls clothed in the thinnest silk and gauze," she told Cranch, were "springing two feet from the floor, posing themselves in the air with their feet flying, and as perfectly showing their garters and drawers as though no petticoat had been worn." Later, she made a confession to her sister: "Repeatedly seeing these dances has worn off the disgust which I at first felt, and I see them now with pleasure."

Paris, with all its faults and virtues, was exciting, but what really thrilled Abigail Adams was the resumption of life with her "best friend." She spent even more time with her husband now than she had back in Braintree, when

The magnificent Louvre museum (foreground) and the elegant gardens of the Tuileries dazzled Abigail Adams when she arrived in Paris in 1784.

he was so often riding circuit or attending sessions of the Congress. The four Adamses ate most of their meals together, went for afternoon walks, and played cards in the evening. During the mornings, Nabby and John Quincy studied while their mother sewed and

Parisians enjoy a Sunday in the Bois de Boulogne, a wooded park near the Adams's mansion. Abigail Adams disapproved of such frivolous Sabbath activity.

their father met with his fellow commissioners.

Because neither Abigail nor John Adams spoke French fluently, they avoided parties as much as they could. They occasionally visited or entertained Benjamin Franklin, but he and John Adams were not good friends, and Abigail Adams found him entirely too "Frenchified" for her taste. Her favorite caller was Thomas Jefferson, the tall, handsome Virginian who had worked with her husband on the Declaration of Independence eight years earlier. Jefferson, sympathetic and charming as well as highly intellectual, was popular with everybody in the Adams family. Abigail Adams called him "one of the choice ones of the Earth."

Despite her growing appreciation of Paris, Abigail Adams was homesick. "I turn my thoughts to my lowly cottage, to my roughhewn garden, as objects more pleasing than the gay and really beautiful one which now presents itself to my view," she wrote to a friend in Braintree. "My taste is too rigidly fixed," she added, "to be warped by the gay sunshine and splendor of Parisian attractions."

She would soon see the last of those attractions. In April 1785, John Adams learned that the Continental Congress had appointed him ambassador to England; he was to be the first American to represent his new nation at the court of George III. He was both deeply honored and somewhat apprehensive. How would the British, so recently sworn enemies of the United States, receive its new emissary? With a mixture of elation and regret—she would miss Jefferson and other friends in Paris—Abigail Adams began to pack for the trip to London. At the same time,

Benjamin Franklin receives a playful crown at a Paris ball. Although Abigail Adams disliked him, the courtly American was tremendously popular with the French.

she helped John Quincy prepare for his own journey: He was returning to America, where he would attend Harvard College. There, he would soon be joined by his younger brothers, Charles and Thomas.

Abigail, John, and Nabby Adams arrived in London in May. The first job facing the new ambassador was introducing himself—and his government—to the king. Ushered into the royal presence, a tense Adams presented his carefully prepared speech. His aim, he told George, was to restore "the old good nature and the old good humor between people who, though separated by the ocean and under different governments, have the same language, a similar religion, and kindred blood." To Adams's relief, the king responded graciously. "Sir," he said, "your words have been so proper upon this occasion that I cannot but say I am gratified that you are the man chosen to be the minister."

The monarch's courtesy was not imitated by the British press, which missed no chance to snipe at the American representative. The *Public Advertiser*, for example, called his appearance at court "humiliating" and suggested that he had entered government service because he had failed as a lawyer. The *London Chronicle* reported that Adams, ignorant of royal "etiquette," had been "embarrassed at his first audience" with the king. Because the Adamses were neither independently wealthy nor highly salaried, they were not able to entertain in the lavish style considered proper for an 18th-century diplomat. Their relatively simple life-style drew additional sneers from press gossips, who characterized the Americans as painfully "provincial."

The newspapers' malice infuriated Abigail Adams. Writing to her friend Jefferson, she called members of the British press "newsliars" whose writings were "false as hell"—or, even worse, "false as the English." Jefferson responded with sympathy and humor. He called the British a "race of rich, proud, hectoring, swearing, squibbing, carnivorous animals" but said they could not be held responsible for their "uncivilized" behavior. That, he joked,

Thomas Jefferson (above) was a frequent visitor at the Adams home in Paris. Already John's good friend, he became Abigail's trusted confidant as well.

was the result of their atrocious food; everyone knew they were the world's worst cooks.

As always, Abigail Adams made the best of things. She accompanied her husband to court functions and diplomatic receptions, took pains to learn the proper etiquette, and wore the elaborate hairstyles, hoopskirts, feathers, and ribbons prescribed by current fashion. In time, she began to enjoy herself, taking particular delight in London's theaters. She preferred serious plays, but she also liked watching tightrope dancers, tumblers, and even a show featuring a "learned pig, dancing dogs, and the little hare that beats the drum."

One performance that truly thrilled her took place in London's cavernous Westminster Abbey. Here, she heard composer George Frideric Handel's mighty oratorio, *The Messiah*, sung by a 600-voice choir. When the singers reached "The Hallelujah Chorus," wrote Adams to her sister, "the whole audience rose [and] I could scarcely believe myself an inhabitant of Earth. I was one continued shudder from the beginning to the end."

Much of her time was spent on domestic matters. The family had rented a large house on the city's fashionable Grosvenor Square, and it was her job to direct the household staff as well as plan meals and arrange entertainment for diplomatic guests. She also worked with her husband, participating in his day-to-day activities for the first time since he entered public life. Because his office was in their home, she was on hand to offer advice, serve as a sounding board for his ideas, and provide comfort when anti-American hostility threatened to discourage him.

Also assisting John Adams was Colonel William Stephens Smith, the New York-born secretary to the American legation in London. Smith, who had been educated at Princeton College and had served as George Washing-

Ambassador John Adams presents his credentials to George III in 1785. To the American's immense relief, the British king received him cordially.

ton's aide during the Revolution, was tall, good-looking, and smooth-talking. He became an immediate favorite of Abigail Adams, who described him to Jefferson as "a modest, worthy man." She was not alone in her admiration for the dashing colonel: Her daughter, Nabby, also found him extremely interesting.

A quiet, attractive, and intelligent young woman of 21, Nabby Adams had been extremely lonely since her beloved brother John had returned to America. When Smith, 31, asked for her

Fashionable Londoners indulge in a game of cards. Uninterested in such pastimes, the Adamses were labeled hopelessly "provincial" by British high society.

hand in marriage, both she and her parents said yes. Married in June 1786, the young couple took a house near the bride's parents. The Smiths often dined with the Adamses, but Abigail Adams keenly missed her only daughter's constant company.

She also missed her homeland. Every time a ship from Boston arrived in England, she invited its captain to visit, plying him with questions about America: What were people at home talking about? What were the women wearing, what new buildings had gone up in Boston, how did the city's common look these days? She enjoyed these conversations, she told Mary Cranch, as much as "a feast."

Another dialogue she treasured was her correspondence with Jefferson, who was still the U.S. ambassador to France. The two friends exchanged family news, gossip about British and French acquaintances, and thoughts about their native land and its current problems. Both were distressed to learn that postwar America was in the grip of inflation. Adams was particularly upset, she told Jefferson in 1786, by the news that the nation's financial difficulties had led to an incident known as Shays's Rebellion.

Deeply in debt and threatened with the loss of their property by court order, revolutionary war veteran Daniel Shays and a group of other Massachusetts farmers had attempted to close the courts by force. The insurrection was put down by local militia, but it left many Americans, including Abigail Adams, worried about the nation's ability to maintain order. Adams told Jefferson she believed such events could destroy "the whole fabric" of the new republic.

Jefferson thought otherwise. He hoped, he told her, that "the spirit of resistance to government" would "be always kept alive," adding, "I like a little rebellion now and then." Adams, who always listened carefully to her friend's arguments, finally conceded that perhaps such actions might be "salutary" (healthy) for the nation.

Of great concern to both Abigail and John Adams was a convention scheduled to be held in May 1787. Delegates from all over the United States would meet in Philadelphia to hammer out a new document defining the nation's government. Eager to clarify his own strong views about government before the convention met, John Adams began to write a book on the subject.

Diplomatic aide William Stephens Smith quickly endeared himself to Abigail Adams and her daughter. He and Nabby Adams were married in 1786.

While he labored on his writing, Abigail Adams decided to visit the ancient British city of Bath with her son-in-law and her daughter, who was expecting a baby the following spring.

As usual, Adams kept in constant touch with her husband. By mail, the two continued their ongoing conversation about current events, politics, and family affairs. They had been married for more than 22 years, but their letters were as full of affection—and humor— as ever. In one exchange, Abigail Adams urged her husband to protect himself against the chilly London weather. He told her not to worry: If he was cold at night, he said, he would take a virgin to bed with him. Then he hastily reminded her that *virgin* was British slang for a hot-water bottle. While she missed her "bedfellow," his wife joked back, she was consoling herself with "amusement and dissipation" in the resort town of Bath.

On her return to London, she attended a series of scientific lectures. She found their subjects—electricity, magnetism, hydrostatics, optics, and pneumatics—fascinating. Listening to the lectures, she wrote, was "like going into a beautiful country which I never saw before, a country which our American females are not permitted to visit or inspect." In a letter to Mary Cranch, she expanded on this theme. "Knowledge would teach our sex candor," she asserted. She realized that an educated female would incur

Militiamen disperse rioters during Shays's Rebellion. Thomas Jefferson, unworried by the 1786 insurrection, said he liked "a little rebellion now and then."

"the jealousy of the men and the envy of the women," but she insisted that "increasing the number of accomplished women" was extremely important for America's future. "A monopoly of any kind," she added, "is always invidious [harmful]."

Nabby Smith gave birth to a son, named William after his father, in April 1787. "I am a grandmamma," wrote the 42-year-old Abigail Adams to her sister. "A grand—oh no! That would be confessing myself old, which would be quite unfashionable and vulgar. But

true it is. I have a fine grandson." Three months later, she also had a son with a degree from Harvard. She was proud of John Quincy but sad about missing his commencement. "God willing, once I set my foot on American ground," she wrote him, "not all the embassies in Europe . . . shall tempt me again to quit it."

She would not have to wait much longer to set foot on that ground. The U.S. Constitution had been completed; John Adams, eager to take part in the new government, had requested that the Continental Congress recall him from England. After expressing its appreciation for the "patriotism, perseverance, integrity, and diligence with which he had ably and faithfully served

Visions of New England's "rural felicity" beckoned to Abigail Adams after four years abroad. She and her husband returned to their native land in 1788.

his country," the congress voted to allow him to return in the spring of 1788.

Delighted, Abigail Adams wrote to Jefferson. "Retiring to our own little farm, feeding my poultry, and improving my garden has more charms for my fancy," she said, "than residing at the [British court], where I seldom meet with characters so inoffensive as my hens and chickens, or minds so well improved as my garden." But although she yearned for "domestic happiness and rural felicity in the bosom of my native land," she had no regrets about her "excursion" to Europe. It had, she said, "only more attached me to America."

Painted in London, this portrait of 41-year-old Abigail Adams was a favorite of Nabby Adams Smith, who called it "a good likeness of Momma."

EIGHT

"A Very Good World"

When the ship carrying Abigail and John Adams entered Boston Harbor in June 1788, word spread quickly. By the time "his excellency and his lady" were ready to disembark, thousands of their fellow citizens had gathered along the wharf to welcome them. Also waiting for the returning celebrities was the carriage of Governor John Hancock, the fiery patriot who had been the first to sign the Declaration of Independence 12 years earlier. The air was filled with the sounds of cheers and joyously pealing church bells. Abigail Adams, away from her native land for four years, was pleased by the reception, but she could hardly wait to settle down in her "humble cottage" in Braintree.

The Adamses new residence, purchased while they were overseas, was not exactly a "cottage." Although it was modest in comparison to the mansions the family had occupied in Europe, the gracious, seven-room residence was luxurious by local standards. From its windows, wrote a delighted John Adams, could be seen "some of the most beautiful prospects in the world." He named the house "Peacefield." The senior Adamses were soon joined by Thomas, 15, and Charles, 18, both Harvard students, and 20-year-old John Quincy, now practicing law in nearby Newburyport. Missing the happy reunion was 22-year-old Nabby Smith, who had arrived in New York with her husband and baby a few days after her parents reached Boston.

Abigail Adams and her husband congratulated each other on their fine sons. John Quincy was clearly brilliant; Charles was irresistibly charming, and, according to his father, the "most of a gentleman of all"; Thomas had excellent "character" and would, his parents believed, soon outgrow his "somewhat wild" ways. Their only doubts concerned Nabby, who was pregnant again and whose husband had shown no signs of making plans for his family's future security.

In the fall of 1788, the U.S. Constitution had been ratified. Now, the nation was preparing for its first presidential election. The immensely popular war hero, George Washington, was sure to become president. The number-two position was open to speculation, but many well-informed observers be-

The Adamses moved into their new Braintree home, Peacefield, in 1788. "It is but the farm of a patriot," said John Adams of the elegant house and its 95 acres.

lieved it would go to John Adams. As they are today, elections at this time were long, complicated affairs, but by March 1789, the United States had two new executives: President Washington and Vice-president Adams. A few months later, the president would appoint his first cabinet, one of whose members would be Secretary of State Thomas Jefferson.

As soon as the election results were confirmed, John Adams left for New York City, then the nation's capital. His wife remained in Braintree, packing furniture and arranging for a caretaker for the family farm. John Adams rented a house on the outskirts of New York (in the area now known as Greenwich Village) and wrote his wife that he awaited her "tenderly." Busy settling affairs on the farm, she did not arrive quickly enough to suit her husband, who badly wanted her at his side. "If no one will take the place," he wrote impatiently of their farm, "leave it to the birds of the air and beasts of the field."

Accompanied by her son Charles, Abigail Adams arrived in New York in June. She was thrilled by her new residence, an elegant, high-ceilinged manor house surrounded by flower gardens, fields, and pine groves. In all, she wrote her relatives, the place was "beautiful," "sublime," and "delicious." Adams was also pleased by her reception committee: Awaiting her were her husband, her daughter and her new

George Washington is sworn in as the first president of the United States on April 30, 1789. At right is the nation's first vice-president, John Adams.

grandson, John, named for his grandfather.

Abigail Adams's life as the nation's "second lady" started at once. Each week, wives of the administration's leading officials were expected to hold evening receptions, serving tea and cakes to anyone who chose to call. Government wives were also responsible for giving and attending frequent formal dinners, usually attended by at least 24 guests. For assistance, Adams employed a staff, which consisted, as she told her sister, of a "pretty good housekeeper, a tolerable footman, a middling cook, an indifferent steward, and a vixen of a housemaid."

Running a large household on a small budget, entertaining constantly, and nursing family members when they fell ill placed a heavy strain on Abigail Adams, but she loved every minute of it. Her family, she told her sister, could "rejoice and be glad" on

Guests relax at a party in the late 1700s. Hosting and attending such affairs was part of Abigail Adams's job after she became America's "second lady" in 1789.

her account. She treasured her new friendship with Martha Washington, 12 years her senior, and she greatly admired President George Washington, who "much more deeply impressed" her than had "their majesties of Britain." The president's wife, said Adams, not only had "beautiful teeth" and a "better figure" than most women, but was "modest and unassuming, dignified and feminine," and "quite a grandmamma."

Whenever she managed to escape her social obligations, Adams attended congressional sessions, which she found much more exciting than tea parties. The accomplishments of that First Congress were indeed stunning.

In only a few months, its members created a national executive and judicial system and hammered out the first 10 constitutional amendments, which came to be known as the Bill of Rights.

John Adams, like his wife, believed that the federal government should have more power than the states, an opinion strenuously opposed by "states' rights" advocates. As a leading government official, Adams was a natural target for political attacks, and his support of federal supremacy drew especially bitter criticism. Abigail Adams was far more annoyed by her husband's detractors than he was, but she tried to control her anger. "Thus it is to be seated high," she said to her sister. "I pray heaven to give me a conscience void of offense."

In spite of abuse from political opponents, Abigail Adams was enjoying life in New York. It was not to last, however. In 1790, Congress voted to establish a new federal capital on the Potomac River, between Virginia and Maryland. Until the new city (which would be named Washington) was built, Philadelphia would be the site of the nation's capital. The Adamses moved to the Pennsylvania city in November.

Abigail Adams found Philadelphia's women well educated and cordial, and she was pleased to discover that the city boasted a fine theater. But its social life, she said, was "one continued scene of parties upon parties," and she had never much liked giving or going to formal entertainments. "I feel that day a happy one that I can say I have no engagement but to my family," she told her sister. John Adams, too, was growing tired of the social whirl, and he was increasingly restless about his position in the administration. Then as now, the responsibilities of the vice-president were light; his only real duty was to preside over the Senate. The vice-presidency, he complained, was the most "insignificant office" ever created.

When Congress adjourned in the spring of 1791, the Adamses went

Martha Washington enjoys a quiet moment with her husband, George. Abigail Adams was charmed by the first lady, whom she called "quite a grandmamma."

home to Braintree (which had been renamed Quincy) for the summer. Although the trip was long and difficult, it was worth it to the couple, who were by now thoroughly tired of Philadelphia, its constant festivities, and its ongoing political infighting. There was, however, to be no escape.

When Washington was persuaded to run for a second term as president in 1792, John Adams felt obliged to stand for the vice-presidency, much as he detested the job. On the eve of the election, he wrote to his wife from Philadelphia: "This day decides whether I shall be a farmer or a statesman. How the result will be I neither know nor care." Both Washington and Adams were overwhelmingly re-elected.

Abigail Adams remained in Quincy during her husband's second vice-presidential term. She had contracted malaria several years earlier and still suffered from periodic bouts

Philadelphia, U.S. capital from 1790 to 1800, was Adams's home for two years. When her husband's vice-presidential term ended in 1792, she moved back to Quincy.

George Washington (left center) and his wife (on platform) welcome guests to a ball. Abigail Adams stands at extreme left; fourth from left is John Adams.

of chills and fever. Both she and her husband felt it was wise for her to stay at home, not only for the sake of her health but because the farm was showing signs of its owners' long absence. The couple's new life-style resembled that of their prerevolutionary days, when John Adams had served as a delegate to the Continental Congress and his wife had taken care of the family and the farm.

This time, however, John Adams was able to spend more time at home. Interstate travel had become easier, his duties were minimal, and Congress was recessed from spring until fall each year. When he was in Philadelphia, he and his wife exchanged their traditional long, conversational letters. After almost 30 years of marriage, the two missed each other as much as ever. Only half-joking, Abigail Adams wrote to her husband, "I have Louisa [her niece] for a bedfellow, but she is a cold comfort for the one I have lost."

In 1794, George Washington appointed a new ambassador to Holland: 27-year-old John Quincy Adams. Sur-

John Quincy Adams ordered this portrait of himself, painted in London by John Singleton Copley in 1796, as a surprise gift for his mother.

Thomas, Abigail and John Adams's youngest child, was 22 when he accompanied his 27-year-old brother, John Quincy, to the Netherlands in 1794.

prised but pleased, Abigail and John Adams advised their son to accept the prestigious position. Abigail Adams would sorely miss him, but she firmly believed it was his duty to serve his country. "At a very early period of life," she told her friend Martha Washington, "I devoted him to the public." The young ambassador sailed for Europe in September. Traveling with him as secretary was his 22-year-old brother, Thomas, who also left with his parents' blessing.

The other two Adams children were in New York. Charles, now 24, was working as a lawyer, and his sister, Nabby Smith, 29, was raising her family, which now included 3 children and an often-absent husband. Adams grieved for her daughter, whom she knew to be lonely and unhappy, but there was little she could do beyond assuring her of parental love and support. Responding to one sad letter from Nabby, her mother wrote, "Why do you say that you feel alone in the world? ... No friend can supply the absence of a good husband, yet while our parents live, we cannot feel unprotected. To them we can apply for advice and direction, sure that it will be given with affection and tenderness."

Meanwhile, Abigail Adams had her hands full running the family property, which had expanded over the years to three separate farms in Quincy. Still, she found time to write her husband about everything from politics and foreign affairs to agriculture to the education of women. Her husband's lonely "bachelor" life in Philadelphia, he told her, was bearable only because of her letters. "I know not what to write to you," he said at one point, "unless I tell you I love you, and long to see you—but this will be no news."

Much of the dialogue between the Adamses concerned the French Revolution, a subject that sharply divided public opinion in the United States. At first, most Americans had cheered the news that the French, like themselves, were rising up against a repressive government. As the French Revolution became increasingly brutal, however, many of its early supporters recoiled in horror. They were aghast to learn of the execution, in 1793, of King Louis XVI and his queen, Marie Antoinette. "I am a mortal ... enemy to monarchy," said John Adams, but "I am no king-killer."

Abigail Adams, too, was repelled by what she called the revolution's scenes of "anarchy, cruelty, and blood." Thomas Jefferson, on the other hand,

Brandishing "liberty caps," a Paris mob surrounds France's Louis XVI. Like many Americans, the Adamses were horrified to learn of the king's execution in 1793.

strongly supported the revolutionaries. His outspoken defense of their cause strained his long friendship with John Adams and completely alienated Abigail Adams. Always passionately committed to her convictions, she told Jefferson that she doubted that they would ever again share "feelings of mutual sympathy."

Political differences also caused a break between Abigail Adams and another old friend, Mercy Warren. Staunch antifederalists, Warren and her husband had scathingly criticized the Constitution, which the Adamses considered sacred. John Adams remained on good terms with the Warrens, but Abigail Adams could not forgive them. Writing to her sister Mary, she referred to them as "my old and dear friends for whom I once entertained the highest respect."

In 1796, the nation's leading politicians urged George Washington to run for a third term, but he firmly declined. At this point, two parties dominated the nation's political scene. The Federalists, predecessors of today's Republicans, favored a strong federal government. The Republicans, ancestors of the modern Democrats, believed that political supremacy should rest with the states. Each party nominated a president and a vice-president, but according to the electoral rules of the day, the candidate with the highest number of votes became president; the receiver of the second-highest number of votes, regardless of political party, became vice-president.

To succeed Washington, the Federalists nominated the obvious choice: John Adams. Pitted against him was none other than Republican Thomas Jefferson. On the eve of the election, Abigail Adams, still in Quincy, exchanged letters with her husband in Philadelphia. "On this day," she said, "hangs perhaps the destiny of America." Less dramatically, he wrote, "If my reason were to dictate, I should wish to be left out. A president with half the continent on his back, besides all France and England ... will have a devilish load." The votes were counted in early 1797: John Adams was the new president of the United States. His vice-president would be Thomas Jefferson.

Abigail Adams was still disturbed by Jefferson's "radical" ideas but she tried to be conciliatory. He was, she observed to her husband, an honest man and worthy of respect. But she could not resist adding that he was still "wrong in politics" and "frequently mistaken in men and measures."

After his inauguration, John Adams moved into the Washingtons' old residence in Philadelphia and impatiently awaited his wife, who was settling family affairs in Quincy. "I never wanted your advice and assistance more in my life," he wrote her. "The times are critical and dangerous, and I must

This Gilbert Stuart portrait of her husband pleased Abigail Adams, who called it "a speaking likeness" of the nation's second president.

At 27, Charles Adams, the "darling of his mother's heart," was a popular, promising attorney; at 31, he was dead, a victim of acute alcoholism.

have you here to assist me." When she arrived two months later, she began to do just that.

Abigail and John Adams had always discussed his professional activities, and he relied heavily on her advice. Never short of opinions, she had given them freely, a practice she continued as first lady. In an era when women were expected to concentrate almost exclusively on domestic affairs, Abigail Adams's role as presidential confidante was noted with astonishment, particularly by political opponents. Without her approval, snorted one Re-

publican senator, "the president would not dare to make a nomination." The senator may have been exaggerating, but not by much. "I will never consent to have our sex considered in an inferior point of light," said Abigail Adams. "[Even] if a woman does not hold the reins of government, I see no reason for her not judging how they are conducted."

The rapid deterioration of America's relations with France's new revolutionary government was one of the major issues confronting the Adams administration. Once firm allies of the United States, the French bitterly resented America's renewed friendship with England, France's traditional enemy. Not only had French ships attacked U.S. vessels, but the French government had demanded a huge cash payment in return for even receiving American emissaries. For a time, war seemed imminent.

President Adams refused to pay the bribe and prepared for a French invasion by beefing up the U.S. Army and Navy. Faced with both British hostility and American defiance, France backed down and war was averted. The French crisis temporarily increased Adams's popularity, but in the end it was his political undoing. In 1798, with his blessing, Congress passed the Alien and Sedition Acts, a series of laws aimed against foreigners and their U.S. supporters. The legislation brought cries of outrage from the Republicans.

President Adams, asserted Vice-president Jefferson, had instituted a "reign of terror" in America.

Campaigning on this issue, Jefferson ran against Adams in the election of 1800. The race was a close one, ultimately decided by the House of Representatives. The winner was Thomas Jefferson. Abigail and John Adams were not surprised; a bitter split in Federalist ranks, coupled with the widespread unpopularity of the Alien and Sedition Acts, had made the election's outcome virtually certain months earlier. Nevertheless, Abigail Adams regarded it as a supreme example of public blindness and ingratitude. "What must be the thoughts and reflections of those who . . . have placed their country in a situation full of dangers and perils, who have wantonly thrown away the blessings heaven seemed to have in reserve for them?" she asked.

In the year 1800, the Adamses faced personal tragedy along with political misfortune. Their son Charles was a successful New York lawyer and father of two daughters; he was also an alcoholic. Suffering from advanced liver disease, probably due to his excessive drinking, Charles, 31, died in late November. Although his parents knew he had serious problems, his death came as a stunning blow. Charles had been his father's beloved "little prattler," the "darling of his mother's heart." Writing to her sister, Adams said, "Weep with me over the grave of a poor, unhappy child," one who "was no man's enemy but his own." He was, she added sorrowfully, "beloved in spite of his errors."

In March 1801, Thomas Jefferson was inaugurated as the nation's third president and John and Abigail Adams returned to Quincy. The former first lady felt no bitterness toward the new chief of state. She told her son Thomas (who was now a Philadelphia lawyer) that she only hoped Jefferson's administration would "be as productive of the peace, happiness, and prosperity of the nation as the two former ones have been." Abigail Adams was now the wife of a private citizen. She accepted the change calmly—but for the rest of her life, she referred to her husband as "the president."

John Adams, deprived of an active political role for the first time in decades, was somewhat restless in retirement, but his wife was more than content at Peacefield, the family farm in Quincy. Much to her delight, her son John Quincy had come home after seven years in Europe. With him was his wife, Louisa, and their son, George Washington Adams. Additionally pleasing to Abigail Adams was John Quincy's election to the United States Senate in 1803. The Adamses' son Thomas also moved back to Quincy, where he married and began a successful law practice. Filling out the circle around Abigail Adams were

Louisa Catherine Johnson, London-born daughter of a U.S. diplomat, visited America for the first time after she married John Quincy Adams in 1794.

Gilbert Stuart made this sketch of Adams in 1800. By the time he completed the portrait in 1816 (see frontispiece), she claimed it no longer resembled her.

Charles and Nabby's children, who made frequent long visits to Peacefield.

The golden circle began to break up in 1809, when James Madison, who had succeeded Jefferson, named John Quincy Adams ambassador to Russia. Although she advised him to accept the post, Abigail Adams, now 64 years old, was crushed at the thought of another long separation from her oldest son. "Of the few children I have had, how they have been divided, brought together again, and then scattered," she said in a letter to a friend. But worse was yet to come.

In 1811, Mary and Richard Cranch, Abigail Adams's sister and brother-in-law, suddenly died within a few days of each other. Mary had been Adams's lifelong adviser, confidante, and dear friend, and her death hit her younger sister hard. Characteristically, however, Adams tried to think positively about her loss: The Cranches had shared many happy years, and neither was left to mourn the other. Her own grief, she scolded herself, was "selfish."

Abigail Adams would retain her strong convictions about people, about politics, about life itself, for the rest of her days, but as she grew older, she seemed to mellow. Writing to an old friend, she said, "As our lamp of life is nearly burnt out, I feel a sympathy drawing me nearer and nearer to those dear surviving friends who began the race with me."

In 1811 she revived her friendship with Mercy Warren, to whom she had not spoken for years. And in 1812, she broke a long and painful silence by writing to Thomas Jefferson, now retired from the political arena. Her regard for him, she said, was "still cherished and preserved through all the vicissitudes which have taken place since we first became acquainted." Touched, Jefferson replied that he wished their friendship had been "sooner revived." He was always interested, he told Adams, "in whatever affects your happiness."

In 1813, Adams experienced the deepest sorrow of her life. Nabby Smith, her only daughter and the child to whom she had always felt closest, died of cancer at the age of 48. She was, said her grieving father to Thomas Jefferson, "the healthiest and firmest of us all." Jefferson, whose own daughter had died young, responded with great sympathy. Gentle, patient Nabby Smith, he said, would be lovingly remembered "until recollection and life are extinguished together."

Two of Nabby Smith's children, Caroline and William, stayed for a long visit at Peacefield after their mother's death. Nothing could have pleased their grandmother more. She loved the company of young people, and Caroline, who resembled her mother, was her special favorite. "The big house in Quincy was like a magnet, drawing in and sheltering children, grandchildren, nephews, nieces, and cousins," observes Adams biographer Lynne Withey. "No matter how many already lived with Abigail and John, there always seemed to be room for more."

In the company of the people she loved, Abigail Adams stayed busy with her domestic work, her neighborhood visits, and her ceaseless letter writing. "It has always been to me a source of wonder," wrote John Quincy's wife, Louisa, to her mother-in-law, "how you write to so many in one family, and yet never appear at a loss for a subject." Replied Abigail Adams, "At the age of 70, I feel more interest in all that's done beneath the circuit of the sun than some others do at, what shall I say, 35 or 40?"

After his wife had recovered from a serious illness in 1816, John Adams wrote to John Quincy, who was now American ambassador to England. "Your mother," said Adams to his son, "is . . . restored to her characteristic vivacity, activity, wit, sense, and benevolence. Of consequence, she must take upon herself the duties of granddaughter, niece, maids, husband, and all. She must always be writing to you and all her grandchildren. . . . I say she must, because she will." He told his son about a party he and his wife had attended, then said, "Bless my heart! How many feet have your mother and father in the grave? And yet how frolicsome we are!"

Adams put up a brave front, but both he and his wife worried that they might not live long enough to see their oldest son again. Then, in 1817, the newly elected president, James Monroe, appointed John Quincy Adams secretary of state. To the senior Adamses' great joy, he arrived at their doorstep in August, almost eight years after he had left for Russia. When she heard his carriage approaching, recalled his mother later, "I ran to the door. It arrived in a few moments. The first who sprang out was John, who with his former ardor was around my neck in a moment. George followed, half-crazy, calling out, 'O Grandmother, O Grandmother!' "

Considering Abigail Adams's declining health—she suffered from severe arthritis and rheumatism—her energy and enthusiasm were astonishing. As her eighth decade advanced, she felt her strength failing, but not even the prospect of death dimmed her positive outlook. "This is a very good world," she said; she expected to "rise satisfied from the feast." In October 1818, she contracted typhoid fever. She put up a gallant struggle against the disease, and for a few days she seemed to be winning the fight, but it was to be her last. Surrounded by family members, she died peacefully on October 28, two weeks before her 74th birthday.

Standing by her bedside, John Adams said quietly, "I wish I could lay down beside her and die too." As time

Abigail Adams spent her last years at Peacefield, happily living with the man she had loved for more than half a century. "This," she said, "is a very good world."

John Quincy Adams (seen here in an 1848 photograph) was elected president in 1825, making Abigail Adams the only woman to be both wife and mother of a U.S. president.

passed, however, he began to take pleasure in talking about his remarkable wife, reminiscing about her wit, her stubborn independence, her courage, and her inexhaustible love for her family. "The bitterness of death is past," he told his son John Quincy. Recalling his departure for France in 1778, he said this parting was easier, because he expected to be reunited with his wife very soon.

In fact, John Adams lived for another eight years, long enough to see John Quincy Adams inaugurated as the sixth president of the United States. On the Fourth of July, 1826, exactly 50 years after the signing of the Declaration of Independence, John Adams died at the age of 91. By a strange coincidence, his old friend and fellow revolutionary, Thomas Jefferson, died on the same day.

Abigail Adams left a unique chronicle of her time, one of the most exciting periods in human history. Nevertheless, she did not consider herself a historian, or even a writer. Embarrassed by her lack of formal education, she thought her letters lacked all literary merit and often asked their recipients to burn them. Fortunately for history, her requests went unheeded; her relatives and friends saved hundreds of them.

Today, almost two centuries after their author's death, those letters provide a unique record of the birth of a nation; of the towering figures who took part in it; of the manners and morals of a vanished era—and of a remarkable love story. The letters also illuminate the inimitable woman who wrote them. Abigail Adams, who once urged her husband to "remember the ladies," was herself an unforgettable woman.

FURTHER READING

Adams, Abigail. *New Letters of Abigail Adams.* Edited by Stewart Mitchell, Boston: Houghton Mifflin, 1947.

Adams, John. *Diary and Autobiography of John Adams.* Edited by L. H. Butterfield. Cambridge: Harvard University Press, 1964.

Akers, Charles W. *An American Woman.* Boston: Little, Brown, 1980.

Bowen, Catherine D. *John Adams and the American Revolution.* Boston: Little, Brown, 1950.

Butterfield, L. H., et al. *The Book of Abigail and John: Selected Letters of the Adams Family 1762–1784.* Cambridge: Harvard University Press, 1975.

Chidsey, Donald Barr. *The Great Separation.* New York: Crown, 1965.

Levin, Phyllis Lee. *Abigail Adams.* New York: St. Martin's Press, 1987.

Nagel, Paul C. *Descent from Glory: Four Generations of the John Adams Family.* New York: Oxford University Press, 1983.

Shaw, Peter. *Character of John Adams.* New York: Norton, 1977.

Whitney, Janet. *Abigail Adams.* Boston: Little, Brown, 1947.

Williams, T. Harry, et al. *A History of the United States to 1877.* New York: Knopf, 1969.

Withey, Lynne. *Dearest Friend: A Life of Abigail Adams.* New York: Free Press, 1981.

CHRONOLOGY

Nov. 11, 1744	Abigail Smith born in Weymouth, Massachusetts
1764	Marries John Adams; settles in Braintree, Massachusetts
1765	Gives birth to daughter, Abigail (Nabby); the Stamp Act is passed
1767	Gives birth to son, John Quincy
1768	Moves with her family to Boston
1770	Gives birth to son, Charles; Boston Massacre occurs; John Adams elected to Massachusetts legislature
1772	Gives birth to son, Thomas Boylston
1773	Boston Tea Party takes place
1774	Adams and her children move back to Braintree; John Adams elected to First Continental Congress.
1775	American Revolution begins with battles in Lexington and Concord
1776	Declaration of Independence is signed
1781	American victory at Yorktown, Virginia, effectively ends American Revolution
1784	Adams joins her husband in France, where he represents United States
1785	Moves to London when husband is appointed U.S. ambassador to England
1788	Returns to United States
1789	Moves to New York City when husband is elected first U.S. vice-president
1797	Becomes first lady when John Adams is elected president
Oct. 28, 1818	Dies at Peacefield, the family farm in Quincy, Massachusetts

INDEX

PICTURE CREDITS

Adams National Historic Site: pp. 2, 14, 76, 90, 96 (left);   The Bettmann Archive: pp. 21 (right), 22, 29, 30, 32, 33, 40, 41, 46, 47, 51, 52, 63, 72, 74, 79, 80, 81, 84, 86 (right), 88, 93, 105;   Culver Pictures: pp. 16, 21 (left), 28, 62 (top), 64, 65, 66, 67, 68, 71, 73, 83, 85, 86 (left), 97;   Library of Congress: pp. 15, 17, 26, 31, 35, 36, 38, 42, 48, 50, 53, 54, 55, 56, 59, 62 (bottom), 82, 91, 92, 94, 95, 99;   Massachusetts Historical Society: Cover, pp. 12, 18, 20, 23, 24, 43, 44, 58, 78, 96 (right);   100, 102 (right);   Museum of Fine Arts: p. 45;   New York Historical Society: p. 104;   New York Public Library Picture Collection: p. 104.

Angela Osborne, a free-lance television producer and director, is a member of the Writers Guild of America East and the Directors Guild of America East. A graduate of New York University, she has written numerous magazine articles for young readers, as well as scripts for Nickelodeon Cable and a young adult novel, *Groupie.* She lives in Manhattan with her husband and two children.

❖ ❖ ❖

Matina S. Horner is president of Radcliffe College and associate professor of psychology and social relations at Harvard University. She is best known for her studies of women's motivation, achievement, and personality development. Dr. Horner serves on several national boards and advisory councils, including those of the National Science Foundation, Time Inc., and the Women's Research and Education Institute. She earned her B. A. from Bryn Mawr College and Ph.D. from the University of Michigan, and holds honorary degrees from many colleges and universities, including Mount Holyoke, Smith, Tufts, and the University of Pennsylvania.

SALINAS PUBLIC LIBRARY

AUG 1995
Received
John Steinbeck
Library